Sea Creatures
in Origami

Other books by John Montroll:

Origami Under the Sea by John Montroll and Robert J. Lang

Classic Polyhedra Origami

A Constellation of Origami Polyhedra

Dinosaur Origami

Storytime Origami

Mythological Creatures and the Chinese Zodiac Origami

Teach Yourself Origami

Bringing Origami to Life

Dollar Bill Animals in Origami

Dollar Bill Origami

Easy Dollar Bill Origami

Bugs and Birds in Origami

Christmas Origami

Easy Christmas Origami

Animal Origami for the Enthusiast

Origami for the Enthusiast

Easy Origami

Birds in Origami

Favorite Animals in Origami

Sea Creatures in Origami

John Montroll and Robert J. Lang

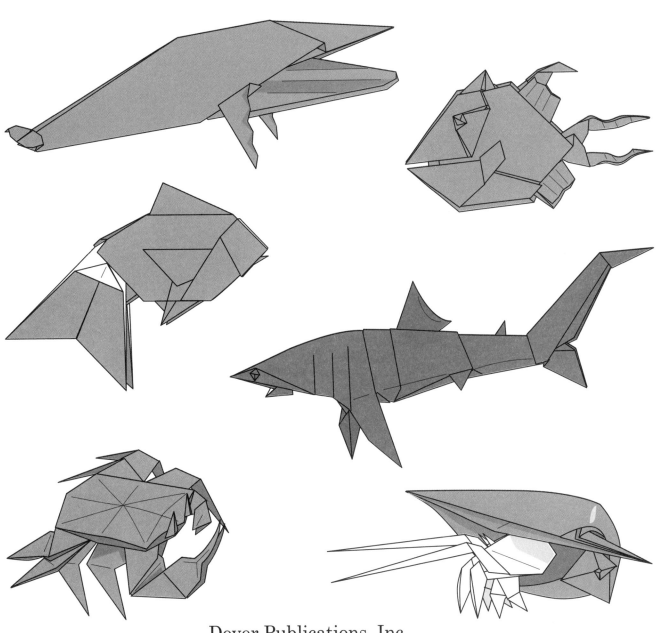

Dover Publications, Inc.
New York

To Heidi and Glenn

To Peter and Diane

Copyright

Copyright © 2011 by John Montroll and Robert J. Lang
All rights reserved.

Library of Congress Cataloging-in-Publication Data

Montroll, John.
  Sea Creatures in Origami / John Montroll & Robert Lang.
  This work first published in 2011 in separate editions by Antroll Publishing Company, Maryland,
  and Dover Publications, Inc., Mineola, New York.
  ISBN 978-0-486-48234-7 (alk. paper)
  1. Origami. 2. Marine animals in art. I. Robert J. (Robert James), 1961- II. Title.
TT870.M5728   ISBN-10: 0-486-48234-0   2011
736'.982--dc22
                        2010048147

Manufactured in the United States
48234001
www.doverpublications.com

Introduction

Fish are hard to capture.

I'm not talking about nets, rods, and reels; I mean they are *artistically* hard to capture. Like most living things, they have a special hold on our perceptions; we anthropomorphize them to varying degrees, assigning them assorted attributes of personality. When we see an artistic representation of a creature, we interpret it not only through its anatomical proportions, but also through the range of emotions we have built up over time and wrapped around the original subject: admiration, desire, fear, unease, even disgust. It is the challenge of the representational artist to evoke some subset of those emotions by his or her artistic creation.

But fish and other sea creatures are, *origamically*, even harder to capture. When creating an origami figure, a large part of the challenge of representing the subject can be boiled to down to structure: achieving some representation of the varied collection of fins, scales, gills, legs, antennae, spines, and more, that go into the form of the subject. And fish, whales, and aquatic invertebrates present special challenges in their structure. Appendages: they have a lot of them. Location: those appendages tend to show up in unusual places, e.g., as unpaired flaps. Throughout the modern era of origami, sea creatures have posed special challenges to origami designers.

In the 1980s, both John Montroll and I succumbed to the attraction of the technical challenges posed by the denizens of realms aquatic, and a chance meeting at an origami convention in 1987 inspired us to collaborate on a book of origami sea life. Part of that collaboration is in this book you now hold. (The rest may be found in its companion, *Origami under the Sea.*)

Both books, together, were originally published as one: *Origami Sea Life*, now out of print. The process of splitting one book into two allowed us to add a few more creatures, some that got crowded out of *OSL*; some composed entirely new for these two works.

It has now been over twenty years since most of the figures in *Origami Sea Life* were composed, and the world of technical origami has undergone revolution: in terms of physical structure, there are no limits on what can be folded, and the armaments of spines, claws, and legs of underwater invertebrates are no match for the circles, polygons, and molecules of modern origami design: given a large enough, thin enough sheet of paper, and enough time and persistence of the folder, any and every one of them can be folded.

And yet, there are still challenges in an origami sea creature: yes, it can be folded, but can it be folded sequentially? Cleanly? From "ordinary" paper? Origami is already an art of constraints, with what we can fold limited by the inherent geometry of the paper. As we add constraints, we focus the art. By taking things away, we can, perhaps, insure that there is more to what's left.

And that, I hope, is what we achieved with *Origami Sea Life*. Even now, over twenty years later, I still enjoy folding these figures (both mine and John's). And I hope that now, twenty years from now, or even a hundred years from now, you will too. Happy folding!

Robert J. Lang
September, 2010

www.langorigami.com
www.johnmontroll.com

Contents

* Simple
** Intermediate
*** Complex
**** Very Complex

Narwhal
**
page 9

Humpback Whale
**
page 12

Dolphin
**
page 16

Octopus
**
page 20

Giant Clam
**
page 23

Murex
***
page 26

Chambered Nautilus Shell
****
page 30

Banded Angelfish
**
page 33

Hideko's Goldfish
**
page 35

Seahorse
**
page 38

Parrotfish
**
page 41

Ocean Sunfish
**
page 44

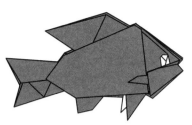

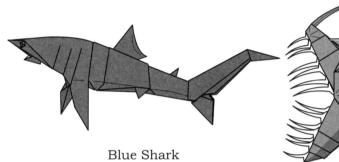
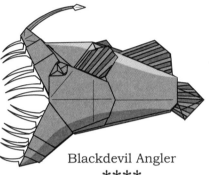

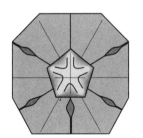

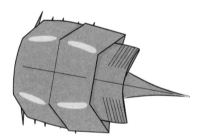

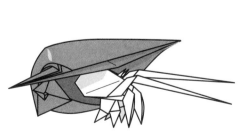

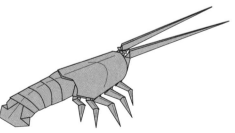

Symbols

Lines

— — — — — — — — —   Valley fold, fold in front.

—·—·—·—·—·—·—   Mountain fold, fold behind.

—————————   Crease line.

···   X-ray or guide line.

Arrows

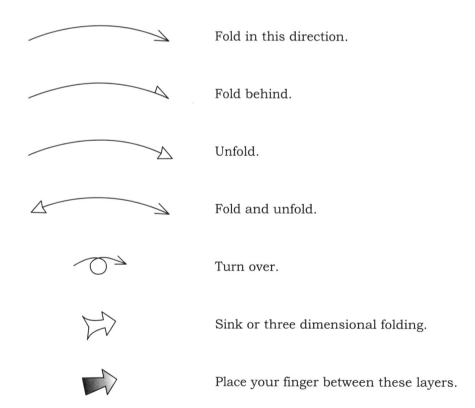

Fold in this direction.

Fold behind.

Unfold.

Fold and unfold.

Turn over.

Sink or three dimensional folding.

Place your finger between these layers.

Narwhal

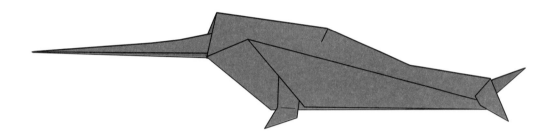

About sixteen feet long, this small whale is found in groups of 15–20 along the Arctic coasts and rivers north of Alaska. It has only two teeth, which grow from the tip of the upper jaw. The male narwhal's left tooth grows straight out to form the nine foot tusk. It eats crabs, shrimp, squid, and fish.

1

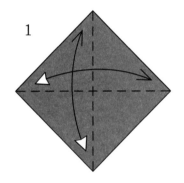

Fold and unfold.

2

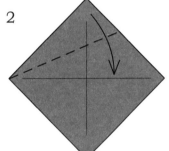

3

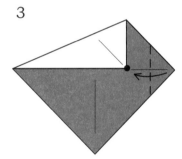

4

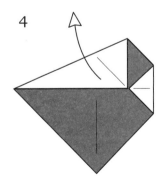

Unfold.

5

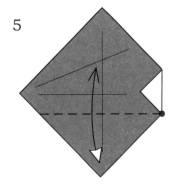

Fold and unfold.

6

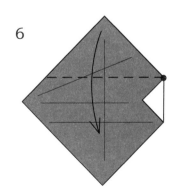

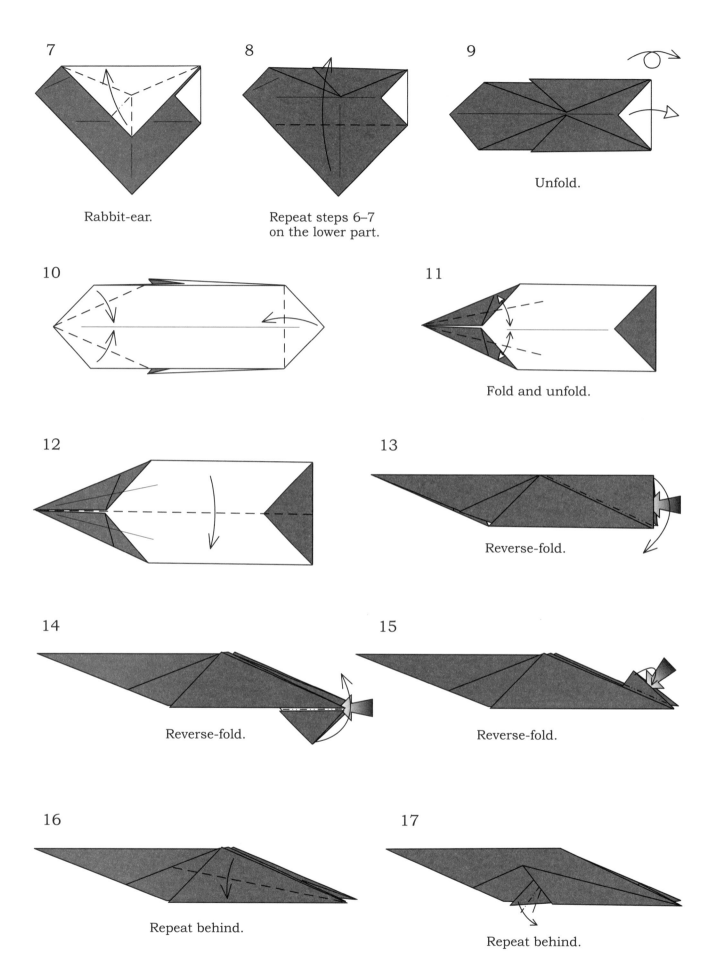

7

Rabbit-ear.

8

Repeat steps 6–7
on the lower part.

9

Unfold.

10

11

Fold and unfold.

12

13

Reverse-fold.

14

Reverse-fold.

15

Reverse-fold.

16

Repeat behind.

17

Repeat behind.

18

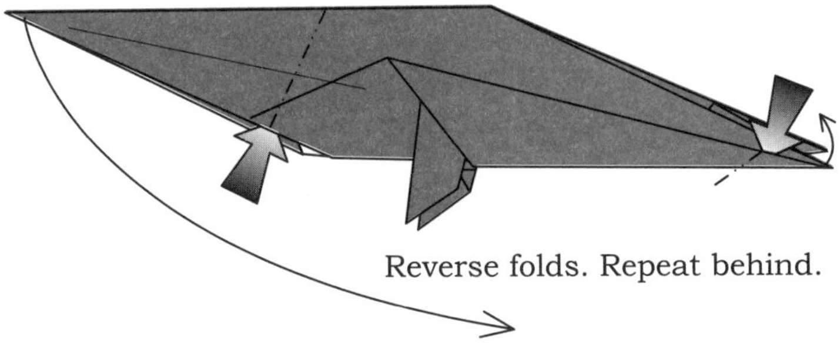

Reverse folds. Repeat behind.

19

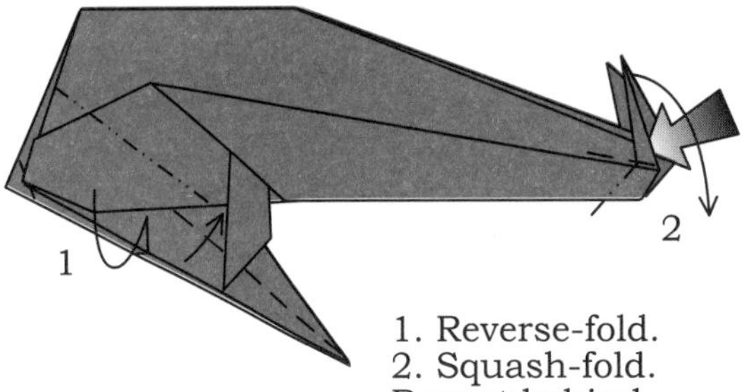

1. Reverse-fold.
2. Squash-fold.
Repeat behind.

20

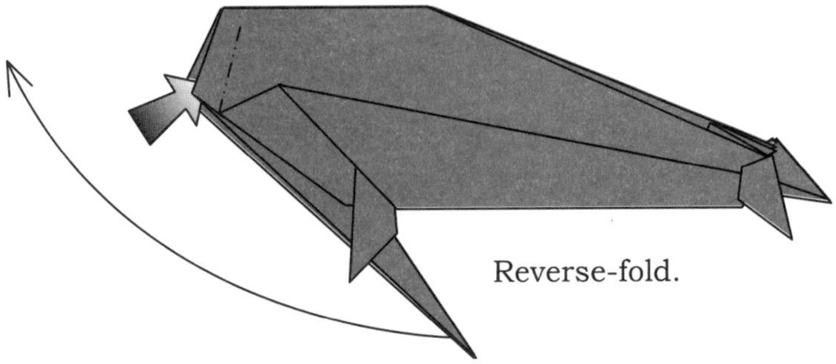

Reverse-fold.

21

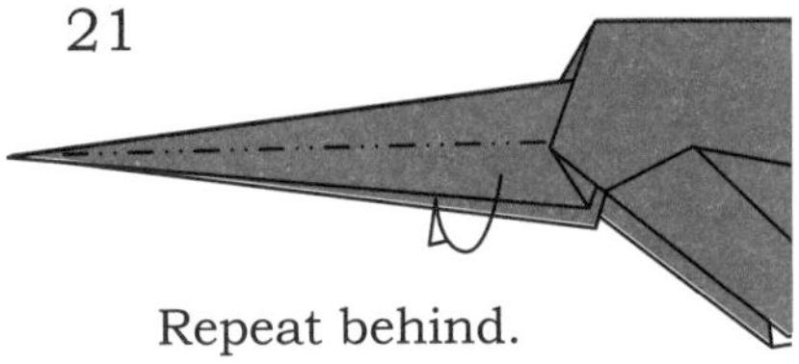

Repeat behind.

22

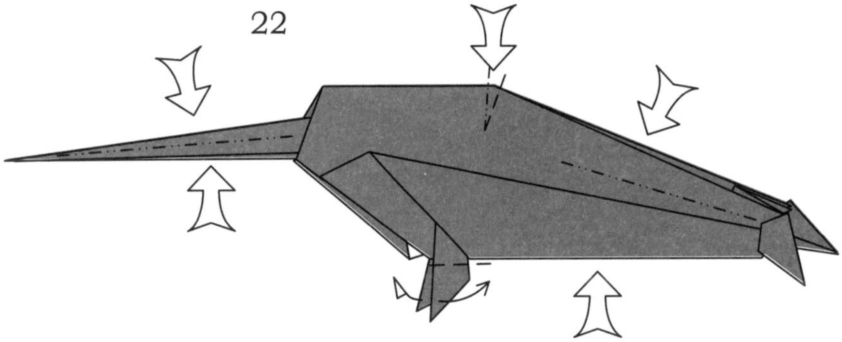

Make the narwhal 3D.
Squeeze the horn to thin it.

23

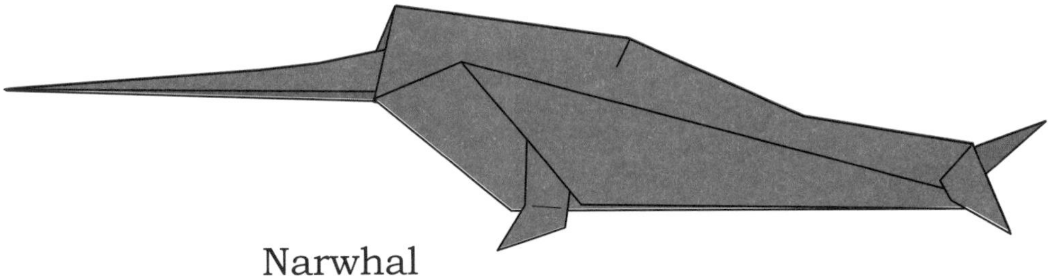

Narwhal

Humpback Whale

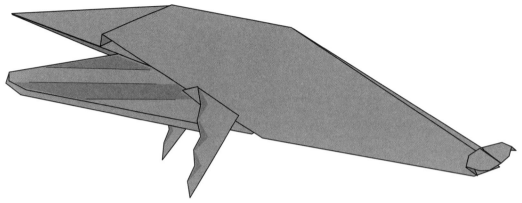

Named for the way it humps its back when it dives, the humpback whale (*Megaptera novaeangliae*) is about 50 feet long. It has large, ragged flippers with bumps along the front edge. This playful creature does somersaults while leaping out of the water. Humpbacks are famous for their long, haunting "songs," which are quite complex. These baleen whales feed on krill and small fish.

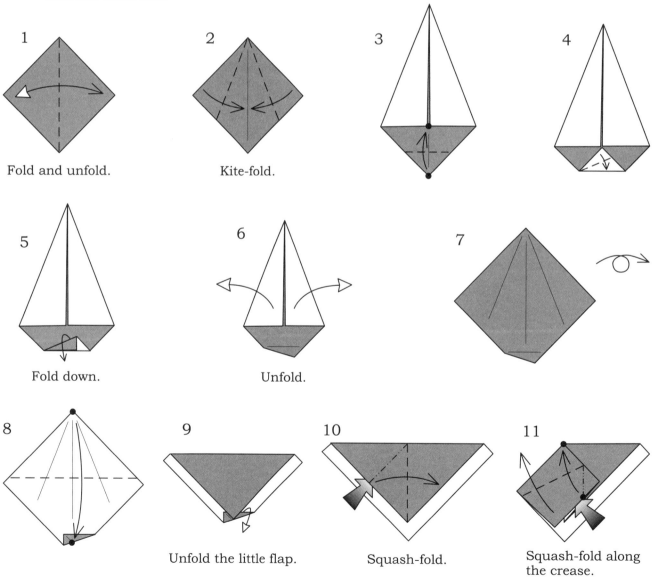

1

Fold and unfold.

2

Kite-fold.

3

4

5

Fold down.

6

Unfold.

7

8

9

Unfold the little flap.

10

Squash-fold.

11

Squash-fold along the crease.

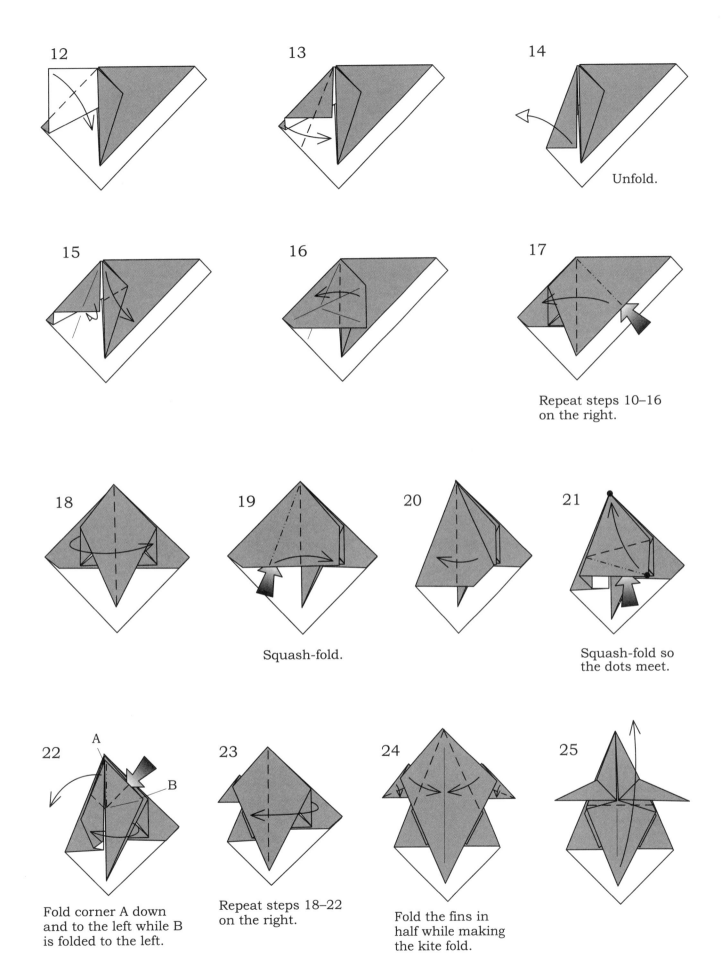

12

13

14

Unfold.

15

16

17

Repeat steps 10–16 on the right.

18

19

Squash-fold.

20

21

Squash-fold so the dots meet.

22

A

B

Fold corner A down and to the left while B is folded to the left.

23

Repeat steps 18–22 on the right.

24

Fold the fins in half while making the kite fold.

25

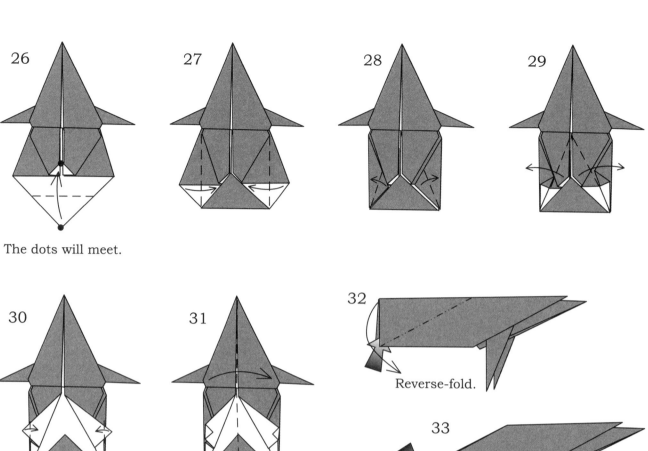

26

27

28

29

The dots will meet.

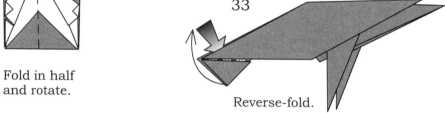

30

31

32

Reverse-fold.

Fold in half
and rotate.

33

Reverse-fold.

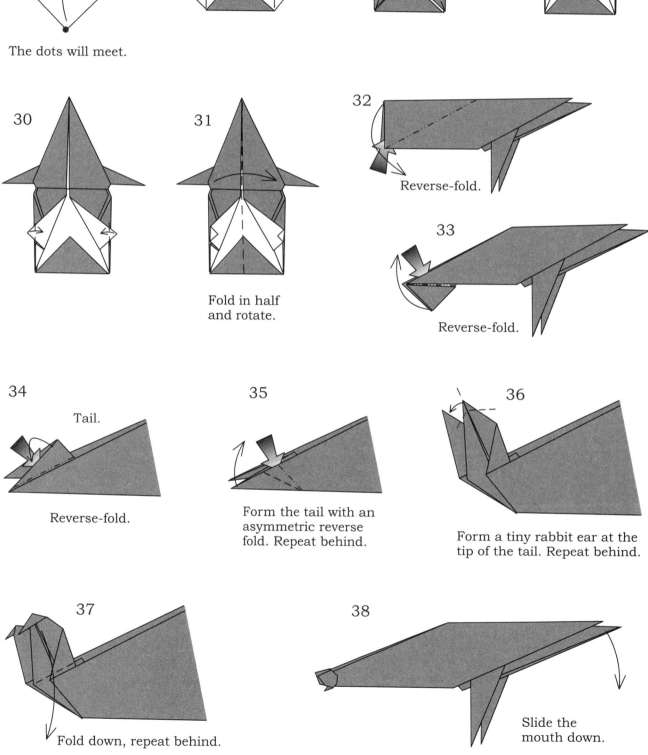

34

Tail.

Reverse-fold.

35

Form the tail with an
asymmetric reverse
fold. Repeat behind.

36

Form a tiny rabbit ear at the
tip of the tail. Repeat behind.

37

Fold down, repeat behind.

38

Slide the
mouth down.

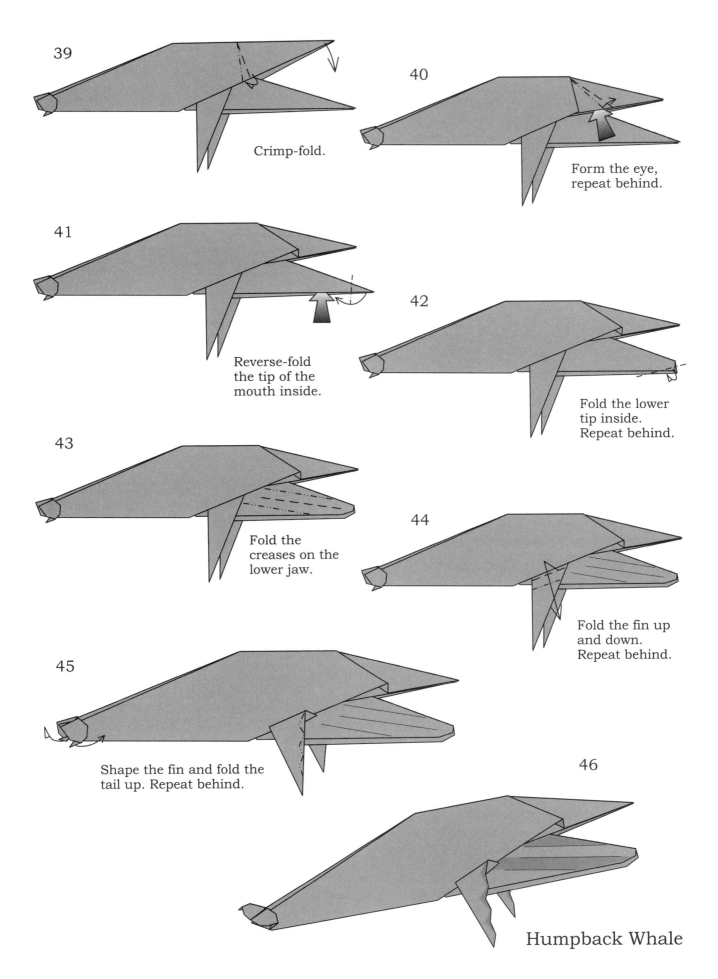

39

Crimp-fold.

40

Form the eye,
repeat behind.

41

Reverse-fold
the tip of the
mouth inside.

42

Fold the lower
tip inside.
Repeat behind.

43

Fold the
creases on the
lower jaw.

44

Fold the fin up
and down.
Repeat behind.

45

Shape the fin and fold the
tail up. Repeat behind.

46

Humpback Whale

Dolphin

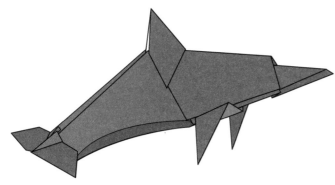

About 8 to 12 feet long, dolphins (family *Delphinidae*) are small, toothed whales. They are very playful and are often found near ships. They are known for their intelligence—dolphins can be taught many tricks—and for their ability to detect small objects with their sonar system. These noisy creatures can communicate by clicking and whistling through their blowholes.

1

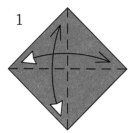

Fold and unfold.

2

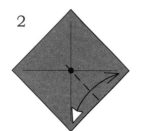

Fold in half and unfold.

3

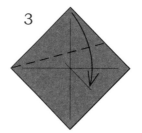

Fold the corner to the line.

4

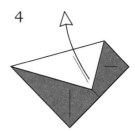

Unfold.

5

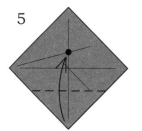

6

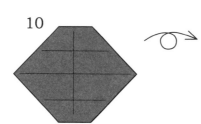

Fold along a hidden crease.

7

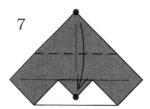

8

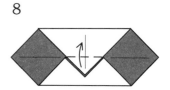

9

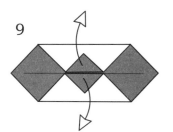

Unfold.

10

Turn over and rotate.

11

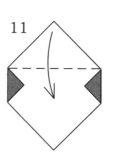

12

Squash-fold.

13

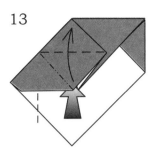

Squash-fold.

14

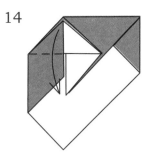

15

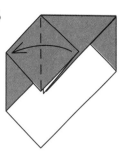

16

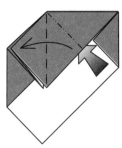

Repeat steps 12–15 on the right.

17

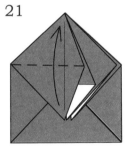

Fold up and tuck underneath the upper layers.

18

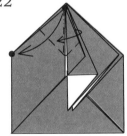

Squash-fold.

19

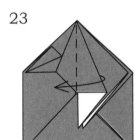

20

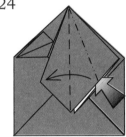

21

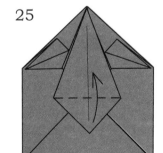

22

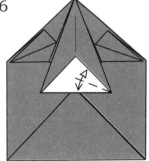

The dots will meet.

23

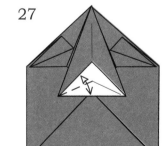

24

Repeat steps 18–23 on the right.

25

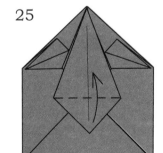

26

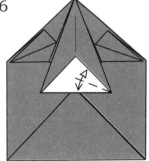

Fold and unfold.

27

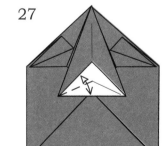

Fold and unfold.

Dolphin 17

28

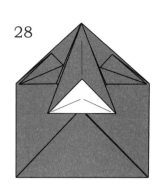

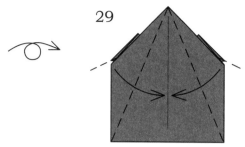

29

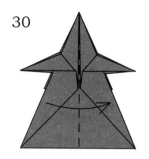

Fold the fins in half while making the kite fold.

30

Fold in half and rotate.

31

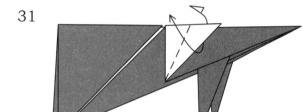

Outside-reverse-fold along the creases.

32

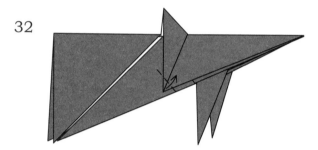

Make a small fold, repeat behind.

33

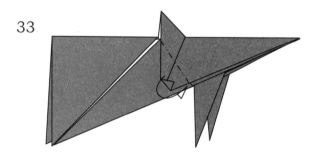

Tuck inside, repeat behind.

34

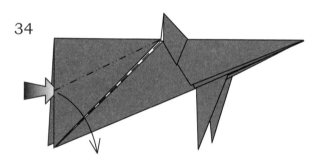

Squash-fold.

35

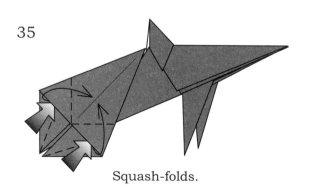

Squash-folds.

36

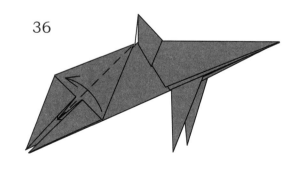

37

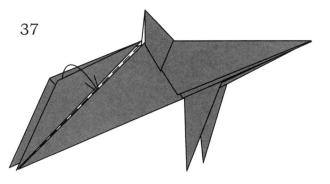

Tuck inside, repeat behind.

38

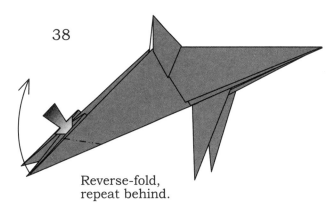

Reverse-fold,
repeat behind.

39

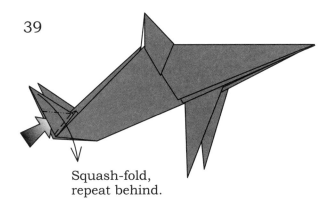

Squash-fold,
repeat behind.

40

Crimp to form the nose. Fold
the fin up, repeat behind.

41

Repeat behind the following:
1. Fold the fins down.
2. Fold the tail up.
3. Pull out a little paper
   by the mouth.
4. Shape the body.

42

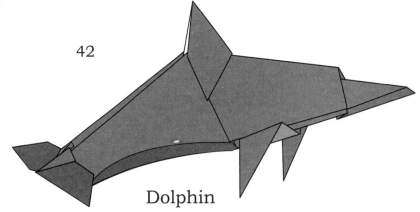

Dolphin

Octopus

Octopuses are unusually intellegent invertebrates. Their eyesight is very good and several species have color vision. The two rows of suction cups throughout their eight arms have chemoreceptors that allow them to taste whatever it touches. There are over 160 species ranging in size from the smallest, the Californian Octopus at under an inch, to the largest, the North Pacific Giant Octopus, which can grow to 30 feet. They live in many areas from coral reefs to depths of 24,000 feet.

1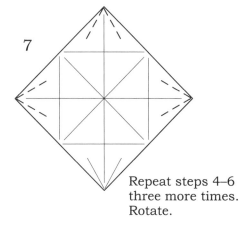

Fold and unfold.

2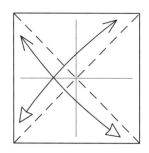

Fold and unfold.

3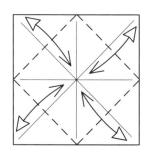

Fold and unfold. Rotate.

4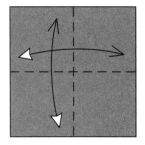

Bring the right corner to the line. Fold by the bottom.

5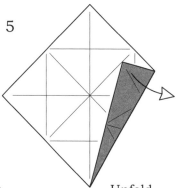

Unfold.

6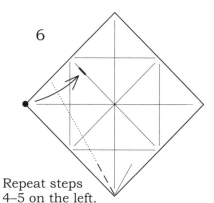

Repeat steps 4–5 on the left.

7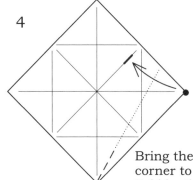

Repeat steps 4–6 three more times. Rotate.

8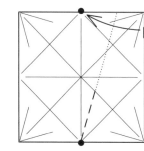

Bring the edge to the dot. Fold by the bottom.

9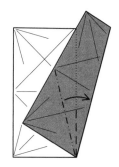

Mountain-fold along the crease.

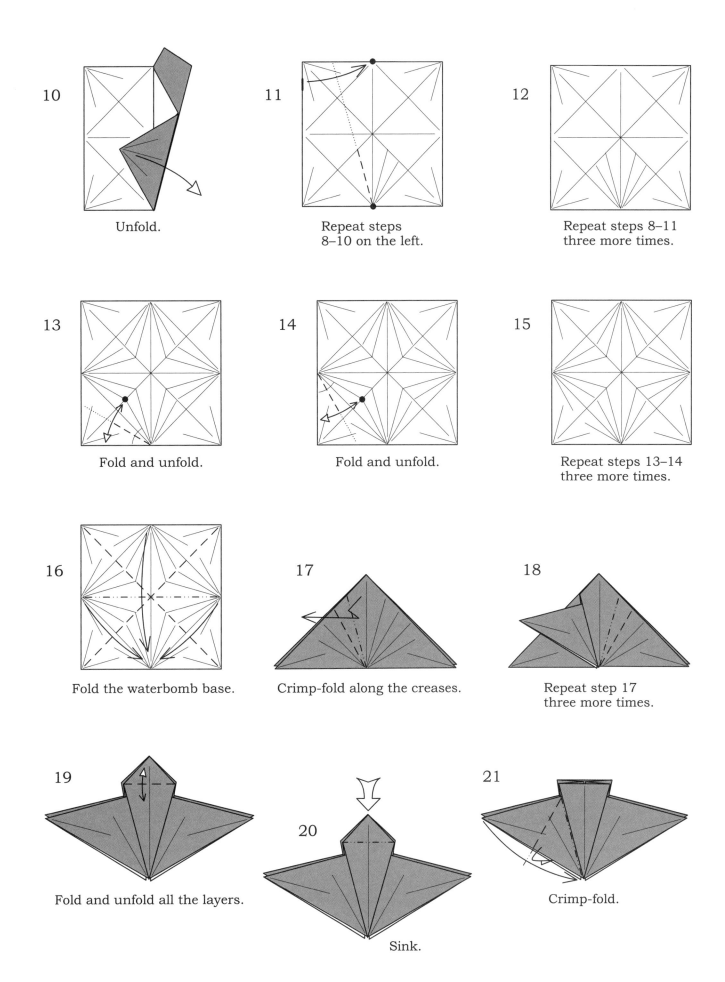

10 Unfold.

11 Repeat steps
8–10 on the left.

12 Repeat steps 8–11
three more times.

13 Fold and unfold.

14 Fold and unfold.

15 Repeat steps 13–14
three more times.

16 Fold the waterbomb base.

17 Crimp-fold along the creases.

18 Repeat step 17
three more times.

19 Fold and unfold all the layers.

20 Sink.

21 Crimp-fold.

22

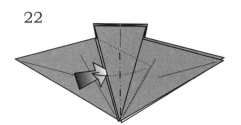

Make two reverse folds.

23

Repeat steps 21–22
three more times.

24

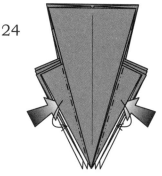

Make eight reverse folds.

25

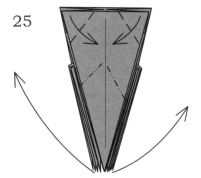

Reverse-fold the
middle layers.

26

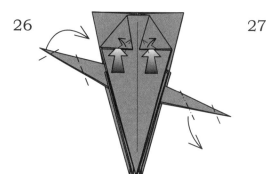

Form the eyes with squash folds.
Shape the legs with reverse folds.

27

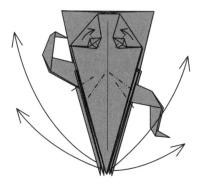

Open the eyes. Reverse-fold
four more legs.

28

Tuck inside at the head. Shape
the legs with reverse folds.

29

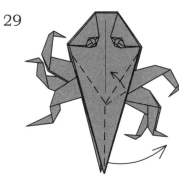

Rabbit-ear with small
spread-squash-folds at
the top. Repeat behind.

30

Shape the legs with reverse folds.
These diagrams show one of many
ways to shape the legs and octopus.

31

Octopus

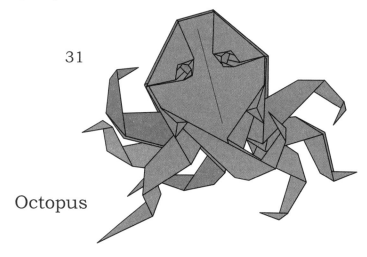

Giant Clam

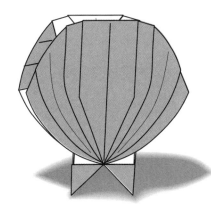

The Giant Clam (*Tridacna derasa*) produces the largest shell of any mollusk, ranging up to six feet across and weighing five hundred pounds. It anchors itself to the sea floor with its gape directed upward and its mantle protruding for maximum exposure to light. It derives its nutrition from symbiotic algae in the mantle tissue, and while it is famous from underwater B-movies in which an unwary diver, stepping into the open maw, becomes trapped and expires, the clam closes at the slightest disturbance in its vicinity, making such a scenario unlikely.

1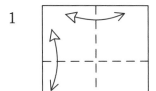

Crease the paper in half vertically and horizontally.

2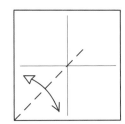

Crease the bottom left corner in half.

3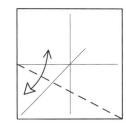

Make a crease that connects the two points shown.

4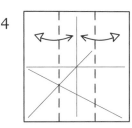

The crease from step 3 crosses the diagonal 1/3 of the way from left to right. Use this mark to divide the paper into thirds.

5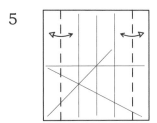

Fold the edges to the creases just made and unfold. Turn the paper over.

6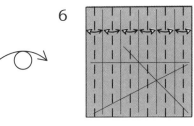

Divide the paper into 12ths with valley folds and turn the paper over.

7

Pleat the sides.

8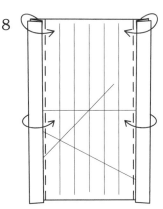

Fold all three layers together as one, on each side.

9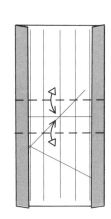

Crease through the intersections of the diagonal and vertical creases.

10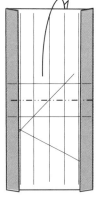

Mountain-fold the paper in half.

11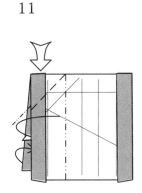

Crimp downward.

12

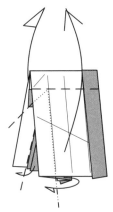

Swing the front and rear flaps upward.

13

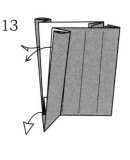

Pull out all of the hidden layers of paper.

14

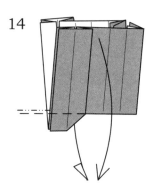

Fold the front and rear flaps back downward.

15

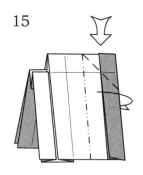

Repeat steps 11-14 on the right.

16

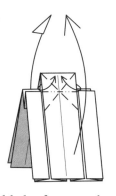

Fold the front and rear flaps back upward, incorporating the creases shown at the top.

17

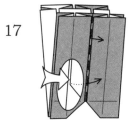

Closed-sink the hidden edge to the right.

18

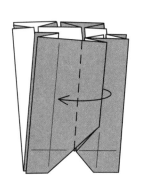

Fold the edge back to the left.

19

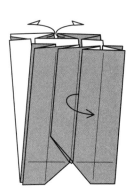

Repeat steps 17–18 on the right and on the back.

20

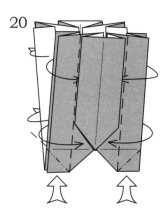

Squash-fold the bottom corners and tuck the layers symmetrically behind the middle edges.

21

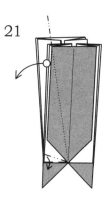

Crimp the bottom and swivel the layers of the top flap to the left as far as possible.

22

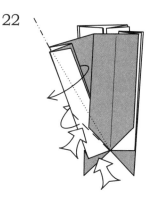

Valley-fold the remaining layers to the left and tuck the crimp underneath.

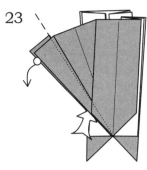

23

Stretch two more layers to the left.

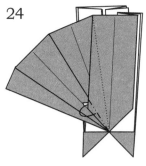

24

Mountain-fold the corner behind.

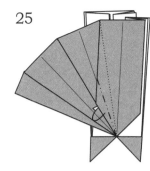

25

And again.

26

This is the direction all the pockets should be facing. Repeat steps 21–25 on the right side and behind.

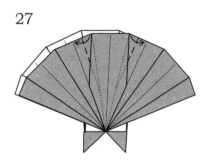

27

Pleat the sides in as shown; the middle of the paper will hump upward and the model will no longer lie flat.

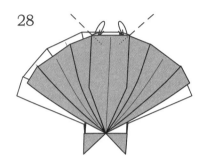

28

Valley-fold the pleats to lock them together.

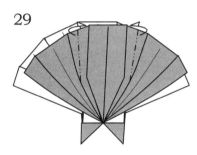

29

Pleat again. The middle will curve upward more and more with each set of pleats.

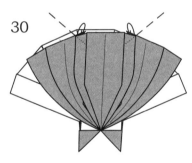

30

Valley-fold these pleats to lock them.

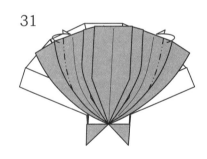

31

Pleat again.

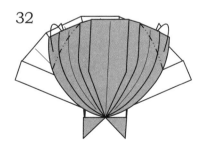

32

Valley-fold the corners underneath.

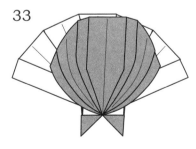

33

Repeat steps 27–32 on the other side of the model.

34

Giant Clam

Pull the two tabs away from each other and the shell will open and close.

Murex

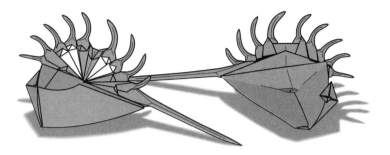

The murexes (family *Muricidae*) are one of the most beautiful and sought-after families by shell collectors. Many of them are covered in frills and needle-sharp projections. This shell, the Venus's comb, has a row of needles along the lip of the shell. Venus's combs are pure white outside and delicately pink inside, and are roughly five inches long. Murexes are found in tropical and temperate waters worldwide.

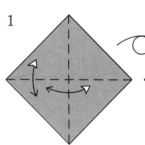

1

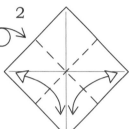

Crease the diagonals. Turn the model over.

2

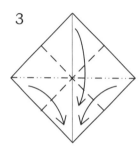

Fold and unfold.

3

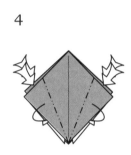

Fold a Preliminary Fold.

4

Reverse-fold four corners to make a Bird Base.

5

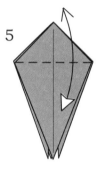

Enlarged view. Fold and unfold.

6

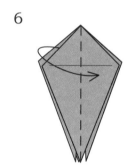

Fold one layer over from left to right.

7

Fold and unfold.

8

Open the top point out and sink it on the existing creases.

9

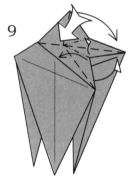

In progress.

10

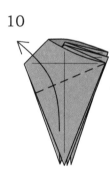

Fold the flap up.

11

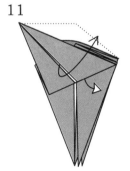

Pull out the trapped layers of paper.

12

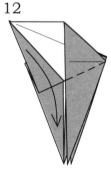

Fold the flap back down.

13

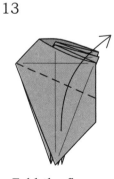

Fold the flap up.

14

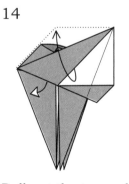

Pull out the trapped layers of paper.

15

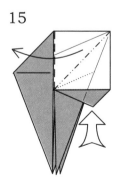

Squash-fold.

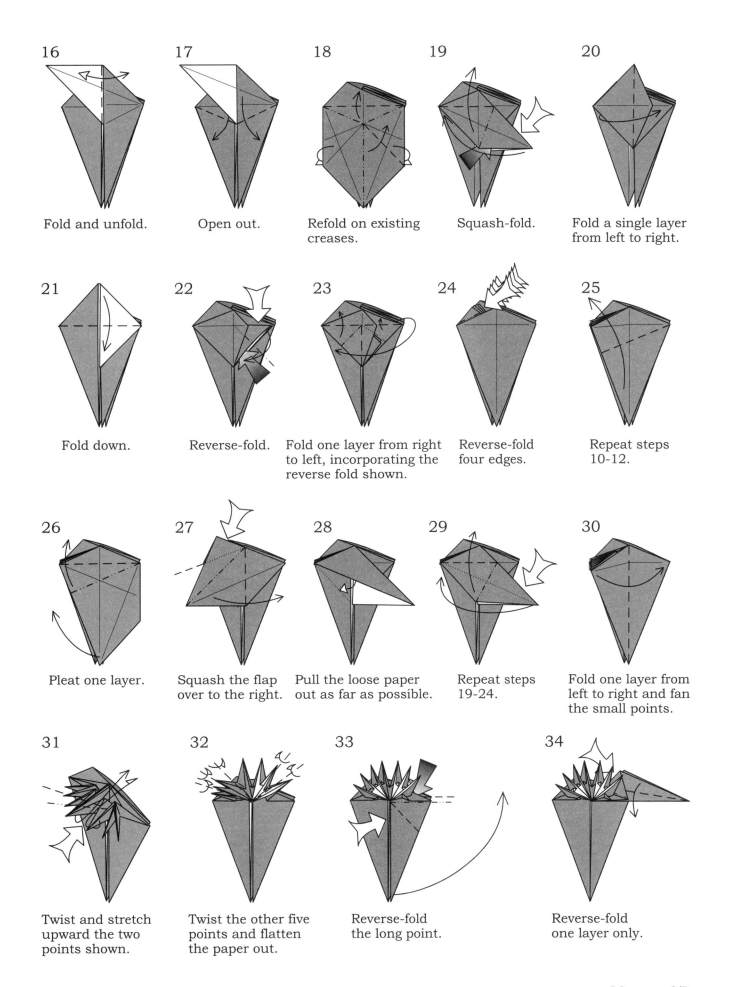

16 Fold and unfold.

17 Open out.

18 Refold on existing creases.

19 Squash-fold.

20 Fold a single layer from left to right.

21 Fold down.

22 Reverse-fold.

23 Fold one layer from right to left, incorporating the reverse fold shown.

24 Reverse-fold four edges.

25 Repeat steps 10-12.

26 Pleat one layer.

27 Squash the flap over to the right.

28 Pull the loose paper out as far as possible.

29 Repeat steps 19-24.

30 Fold one layer from left to right and fan the small points.

31 Twist and stretch upward the two points shown.

32 Twist the other five points and flatten the paper out.

33 Reverse-fold the long point.

34 Reverse-fold one layer only.

35

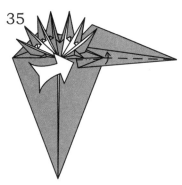

Reverse-fold.

36

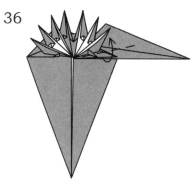

Twist the remaining point upward.

37

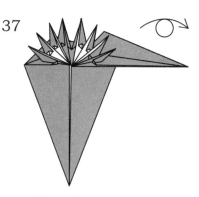

Turn the paper over.

38

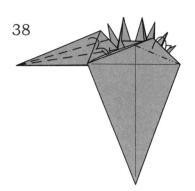

Fold the long edge over and over and tuck it into the pocket.

39

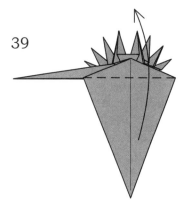

Lift up the remaining long flap.

40

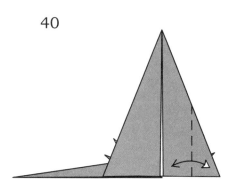

Enlarged view. Fold the corner in and unfold.

41

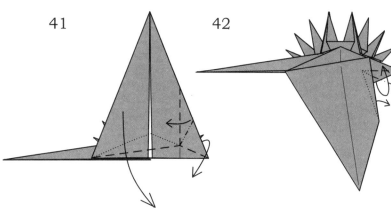

Rabbit-ear the flap, using existing creases.

42

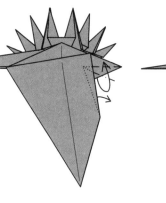

Swivel fold.

43

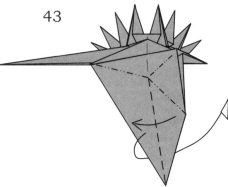

Fold the tip of the point in half and swing it up to the right. Make the mountain folds soft.

44

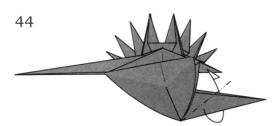

Mountain-fold the point behind.

45

Again.

46

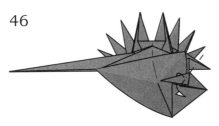

Continue until you run out of point.

47

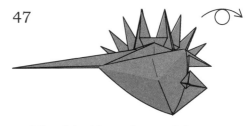

Like this. Turn the model over.

48

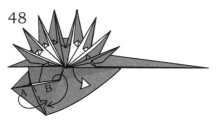

Pull the loose paper out as far as possible and bring points A and B together.

49

Push the shell in here.

50

Pinch all of the points.

51

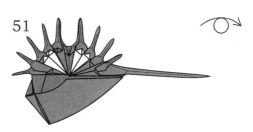

Like this. Turn the paper over.

52

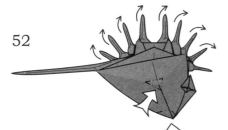

Curve the points. Sink the corners of the shell.

53

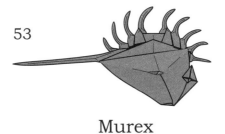

Murex

Chambered Nautilus Shell

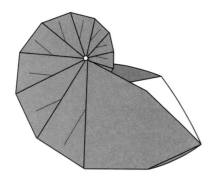

The Chambered Nautilus (*Nautilus pompilius*) is one of the oldest of the cephalopods, a group that includes the octopus and squid. It is highly valued for its symmetric shell, which forms a logarithmic spiral in cross section. The Nautilus is native to the Indian and Pacific Oceans.

1
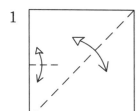

Crease the diagonal of the square and make a pinch mark along the left side halfway up.

2
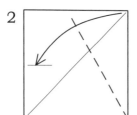

Fold the top right corner down to the pinch mark you just made.

3
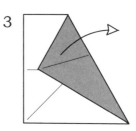

Unfold.

4
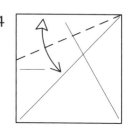

Fold the top edge down to lie along the diagonal.

5
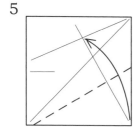

Fold the bottom right corner up to touch the intersection of the last two creases.

6
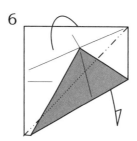

Fold the corner behind along the diagonal of the square.

7
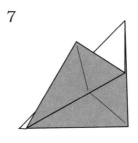

Like this. Turn the paper over.

8
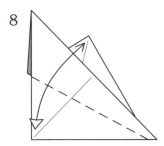

Fold the bottom left corner up to match the one behind and unfold.

9
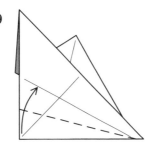

Fold the edge up to touch the crease you just made.

10
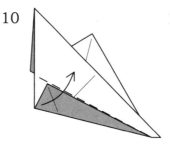

Fold up on the existing crease.

11
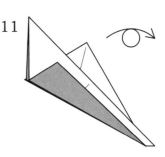

Turn the paper over.

12

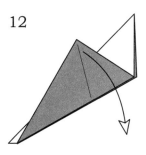

Unfold this flap and repeat steps 9–10.

13

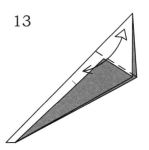

Fold and unfold.

14

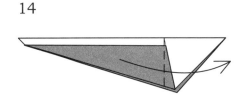

Fold the left point over to the right so that the top edges of the point are aligned.

15

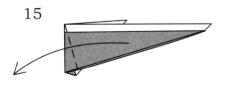

Fold the point back to the left so that the bottom edges of the point are aligned.

16

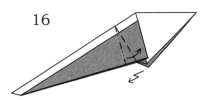

Repeat steps 14–15. Note the location of the valley fold.

17

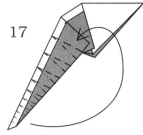

Continue pleating as in steps 14–15 until you get to the end of the colored part of the point (for a total of about 12 or13 pleats).

18

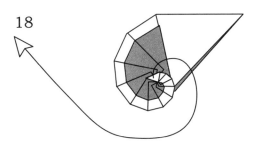

Like this. Unfold to step 13.

19

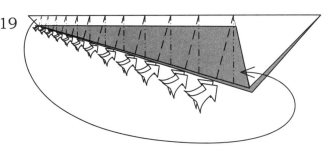

Using the existing creases, crimp both of the bottom edges so that the paper coils up again. The colored flap on the front (and the corresponding one on the back) should not be trapped in the pleats of the white layer; see step 20 for the crease pattern.

20

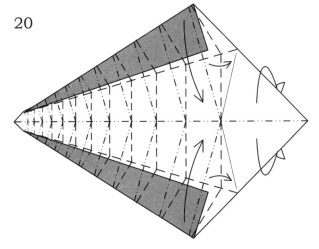

This shows the crease pattern for step 19.

21

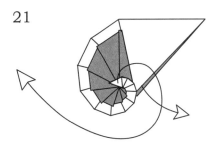

Unfold again to step 13 and open the model out flat.

22

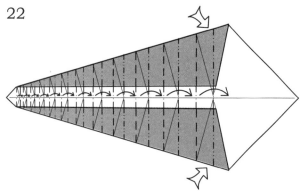

Using the existing creases as guides, crimp the point to the right, folding it in and out (push arrows are shown only for the first crimp).

23

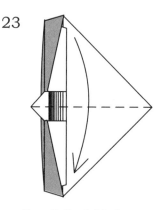

Carefully fold the paper in half through the thick layers.

24

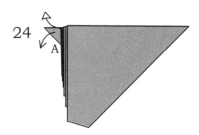

Carefully pull out the top of the protruding point and pivot it downward, taking point A as the axis of rotation. This has the effect of restoring a crimp we made in step 20.

25

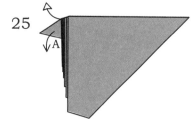

Now, carefully grasp that crimp and pull it out, again pivoting around point A; the result restores the next crimp.

26

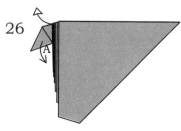

Continue pulling each crimp out and pivoting around point A. The paper remains locked together at point A at all crimps.

27

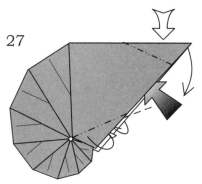

Reverse-fold the top corner. Mountain-fold the corners at the pivot point. Repeat behind.

28

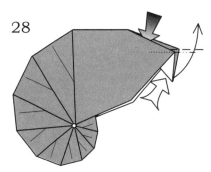

Reverse-fold the corner back up.

29

Sink the hidden corner.

30

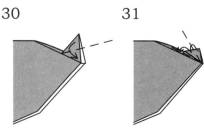

Fold the tip down.

31

Fold the point over and over and tuck it into the pocket.

32

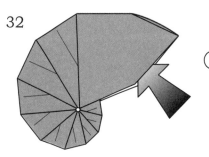

Open out the shell and turn it over.

33

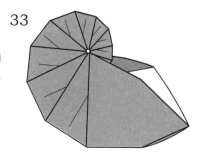

Chambered Nautilus Shell

Banded Angelfish

The Angelfish (genus *Pterophyllum*) are a group of popular aquarium fish noted for their distinctive triangular shape and, often, striking vertical colored bands.

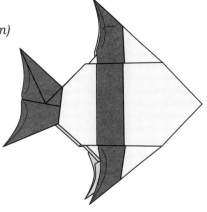

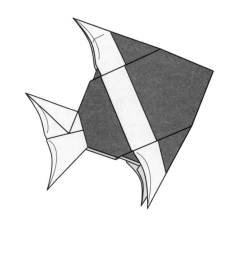

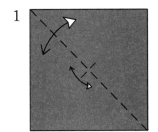
1 Colored side up. Fold and unfold along one diagonal and pinch along the other.

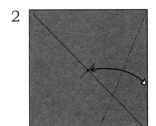
2 Fold and unfold, making a pinch along the bottom.

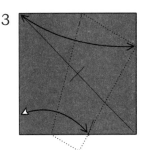
3 Align the indicated points and make a pinch along the top.

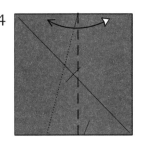
4 Fold and unfold through the pinch.

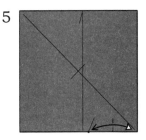
5 Fold the corner to the pinch and unfold.

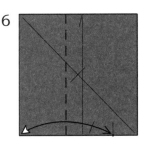
6 Fold the corner to the pinch and unfold.

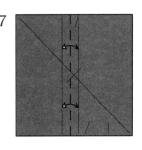
7 Fold and unfold.

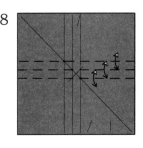
8 Fold and unfold three places.

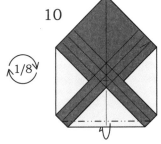
9 Fold three corners in. Rotate 1/8 turn.

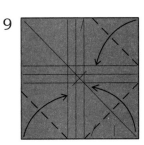
10 Mountain-fold the bottom edge behind.

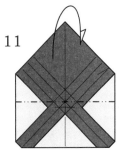
11 Mountain-fold the top behind through the indicated point.

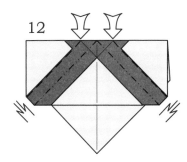
12 Crimp on existing creases.

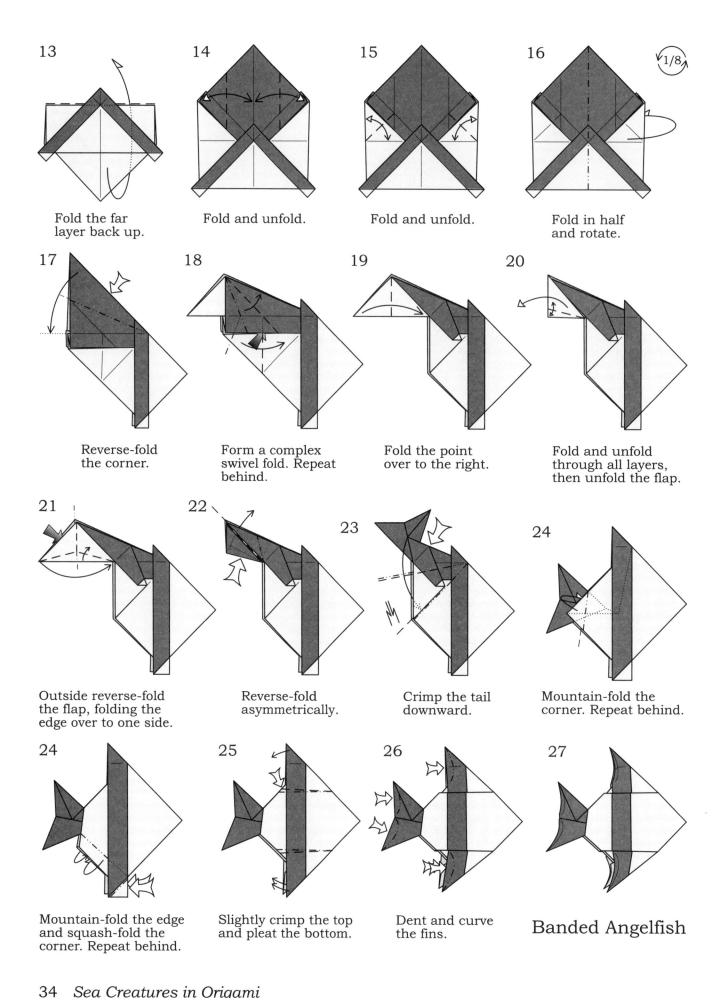

13

Fold the far
layer back up.

14

Fold and unfold.

15

Fold and unfold.

16 ↙1/8↗

Fold in half
and rotate.

17

Reverse-fold
the corner.

18

Form a complex
swivel fold. Repeat
behind.

19

Fold the point
over to the right.

20

Fold and unfold
through all layers,
then unfold the flap.

21

Outside reverse-fold
the flap, folding the
edge over to one side.

22

Reverse-fold
asymmetrically.

23

Crimp the tail
downward.

24

Mountain-fold the
corner. Repeat behind.

24

Mountain-fold the edge
and squash-fold the
corner. Repeat behind.

25

Slightly crimp the top
and pleat the bottom.

26

Dent and curve
the fins.

27

Banded Angelfish

Hideko's Goldfish

Goldfish are decorative freshwater fish that are one of the earliest fish to be domesticated. They are relatives of carp, and now come in a wide array of colors and conformations. This fish is a more realistic variation of Tokinobu's Goldfish, which was a one-piece version of a traditional Japanese cut design.

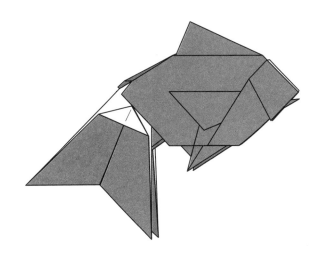

1

Fold and unfold.

2

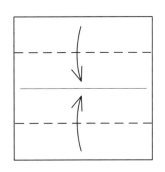

3

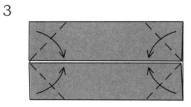

4

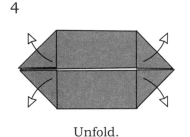

Unfold.

5

Make reverse folds.

6

7

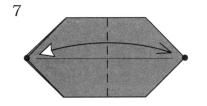

Fold and unfold.

8

9

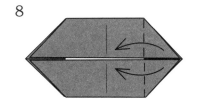

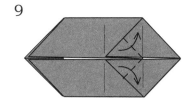

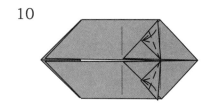

11

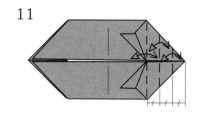

Fold and unfold in thirds.

12

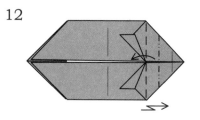

Pleat.

13

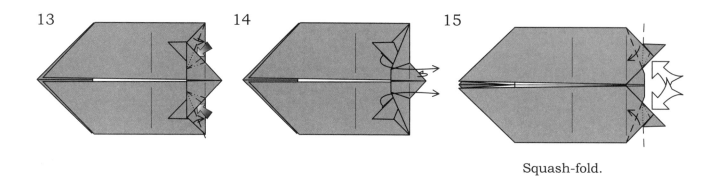

14

15

Squash-fold.

16

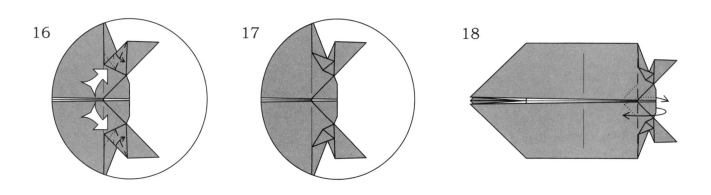

17

18

19

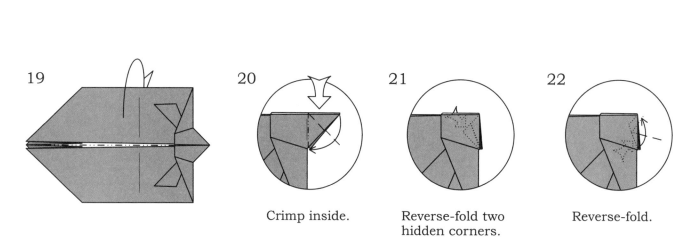

20

Crimp inside.

21

Reverse-fold two
hidden corners.

22

Reverse-fold.

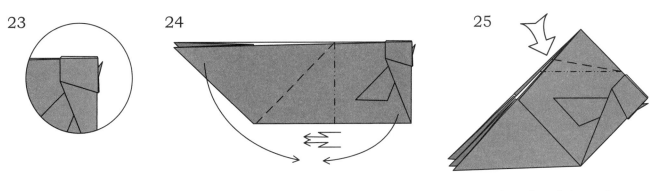

23

24

25

Closed-sink in and out.

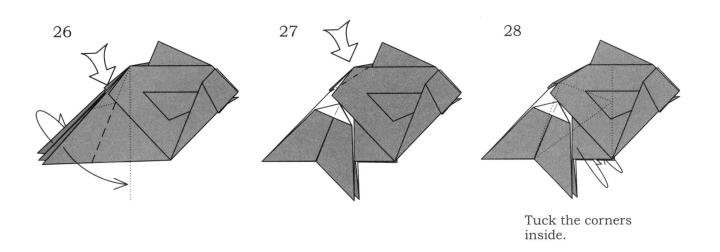

26

27

28

Tuck the corners inside.

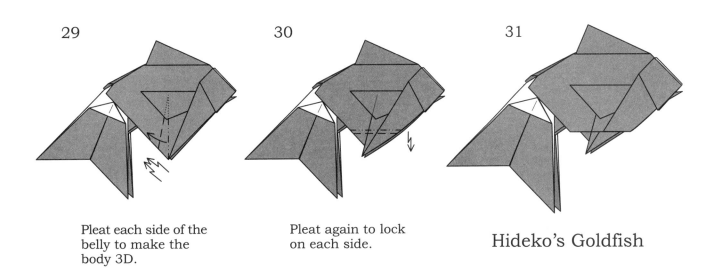

29

Pleat each side of the belly to make the body 3D.

30

Pleat again to lock on each side.

31

Hideko's Goldfish

Seahorse

These small fish are mostly found in subtropical and tropical seas. They attach themselves to seaweed with their prehensile tails. Slowly and stiffly, they swim in an upright position. Their small scales form rings of hard protective covering around their bodies. Ranging in size from one and a half to twelve inches, seahorses (family *Hippocampus*) feed on small crustaceans and larvae.

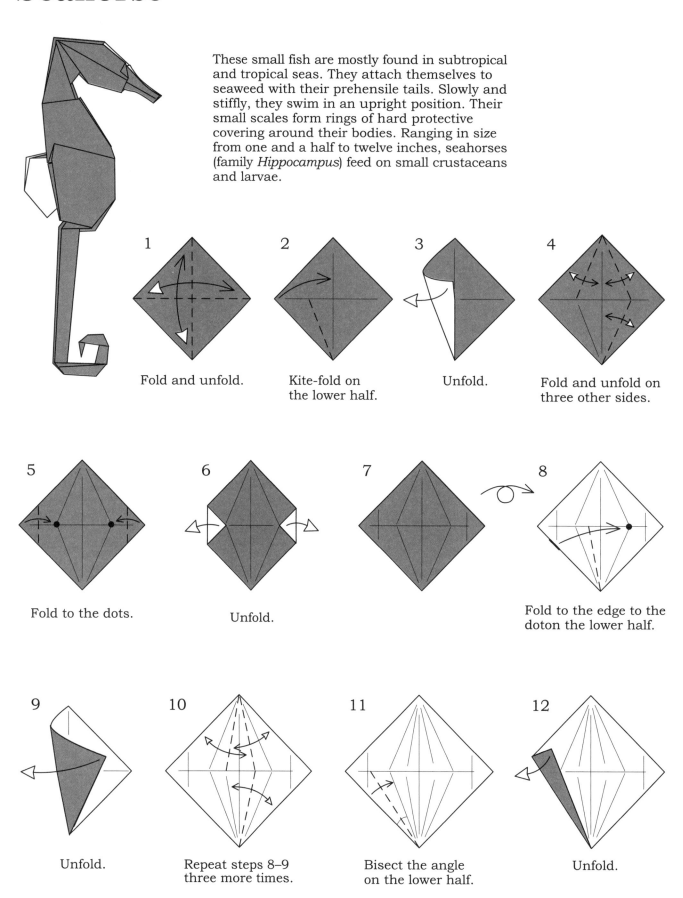

1

Fold and unfold.

2

Kite-fold on the lower half.

3

Unfold.

4

Fold and unfold on three other sides.

5

Fold to the dots.

6

Unfold.

7

8

Fold to the edge to the dot on the lower half.

9

Unfold.

10

Repeat steps 8–9 three more times.

11

Bisect the angle on the lower half.

12

Unfold.

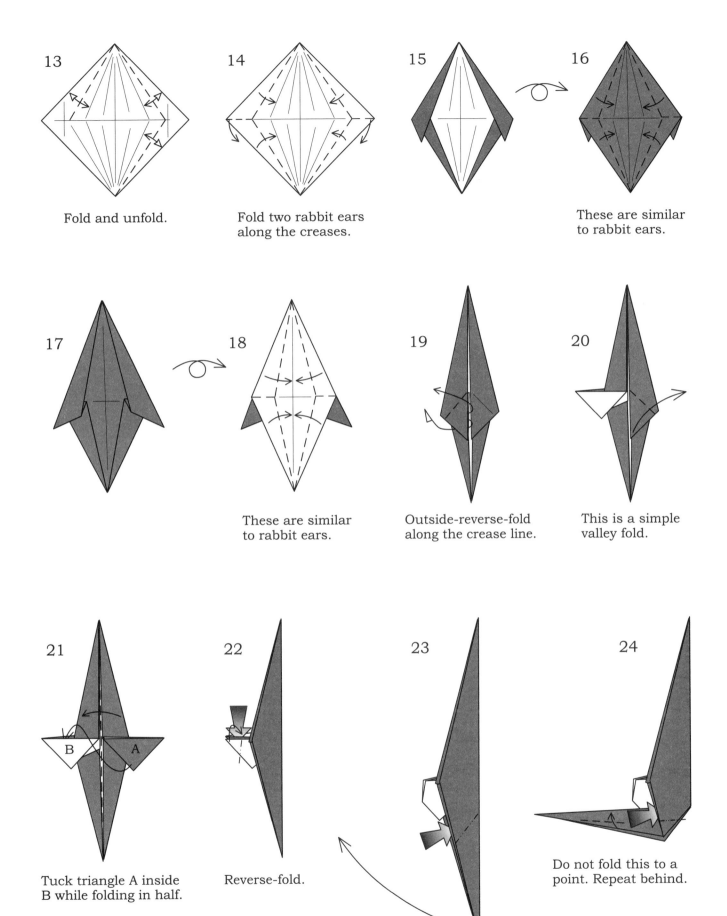

13 Fold and unfold.

14 Fold two rabbit ears along the creases.

15

16 These are similar to rabbit ears.

17

18 These are similar to rabbit ears.

19 Outside-reverse-fold along the crease line.

20 This is a simple valley fold.

21 Tuck triangle A inside B while folding in half.

22 Reverse-fold.

23

Reverse-fold.

24 Do not fold this to a point. Repeat behind.

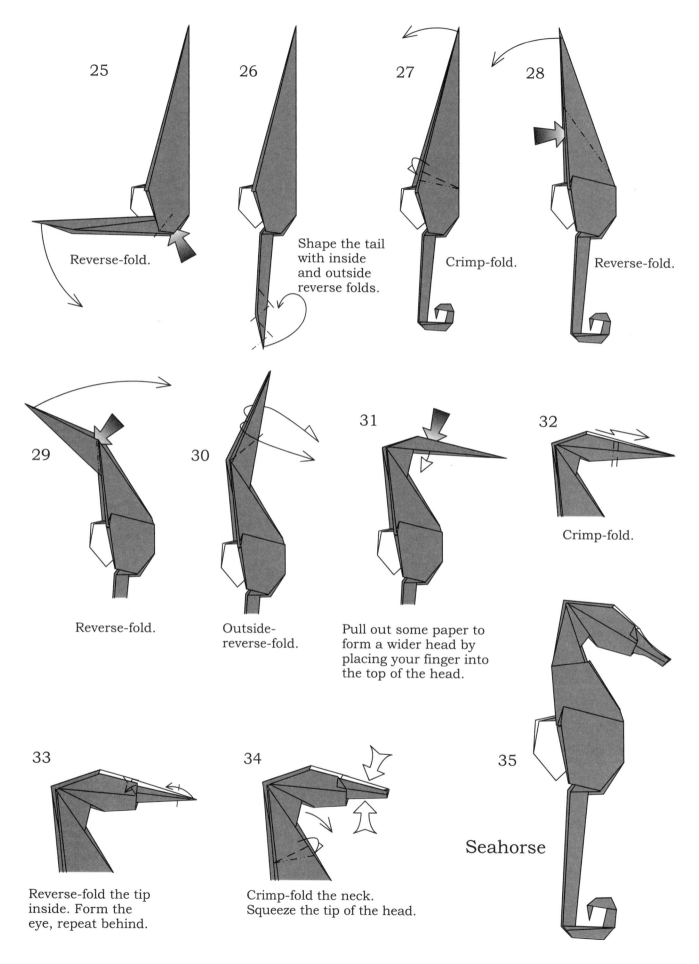

25

Reverse-fold.

26

Shape the tail
with inside
and outside
reverse folds.

27

Crimp-fold.

28

Reverse-fold.

29

Reverse-fold.

30

Outside-
reverse-fold.

31

Pull out some paper to
form a wider head by
placing your finger into
the top of the head.

32

Crimp-fold.

33

Reverse-fold the tip
inside. Form the
eye, repeat behind.

34

Crimp-fold the neck.
Squeeze the tip of the head.

35

Seahorse

Parrotfish

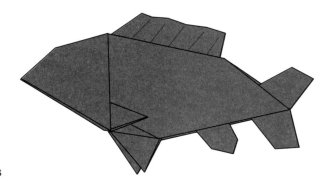

Parrotfishes (*Scaridae*) are found around the world, often in shallow tropical waters, coral reefs, and seagrass beds. Their teeth resemble a parrot's beak. They feed on algae which they extract from coral. They are about 12 to 20 inches long. They are brightly colored and their coloring changes throughout their lives.

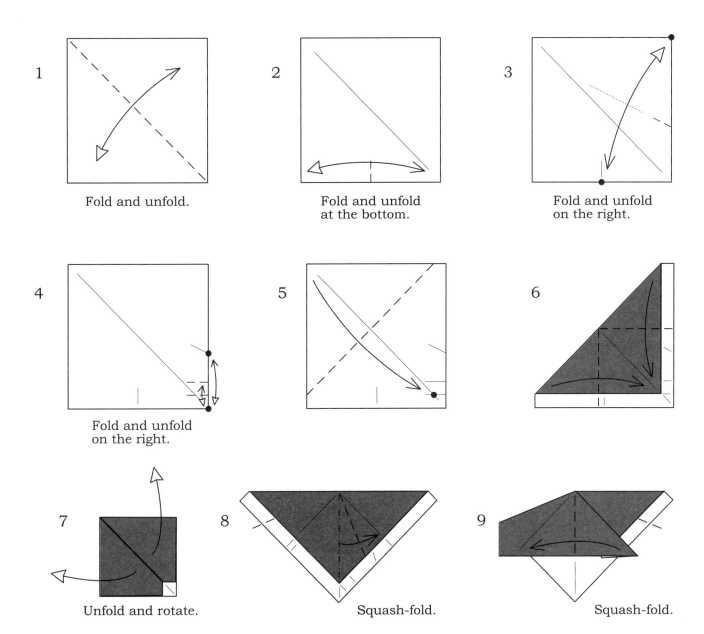

1   Fold and unfold.

2   Fold and unfold at the bottom.

3   Fold and unfold on the right.

4   Fold and unfold on the right.

5

6

7   Unfold and rotate.

8   Squash-fold.

9   Squash-fold.

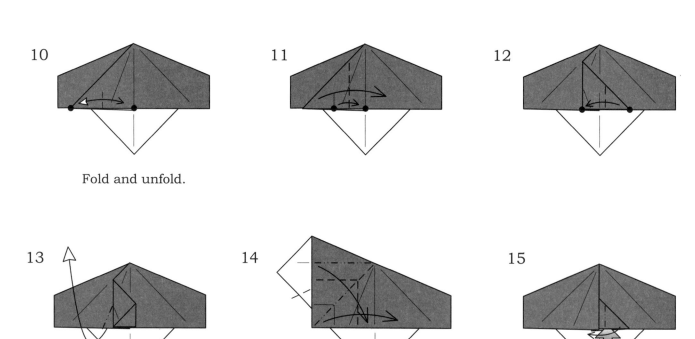

10   Fold and unfold.

11

12

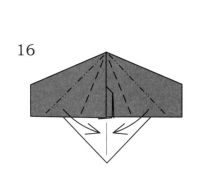

13   Unfold.

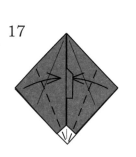

14   Fold along the creases.

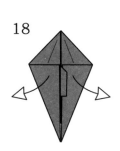

15   Reverse-fold along the crease.

16

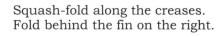

Squash-fold along the creases.
Fold behind the fin on the right.

17   Kite-fold.

18   Unfold.

19

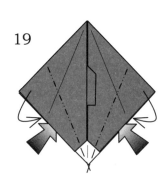

Reverse folds.

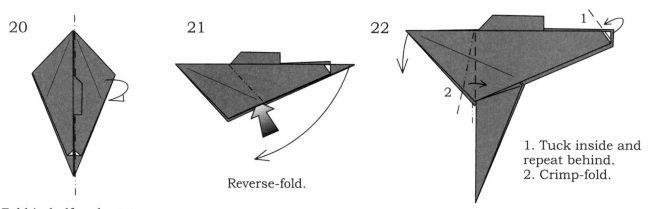

20   Fold in half and rotate.

21   Reverse-fold.

22   1. Tuck inside and repeat behind.
2. Crimp-fold.

23

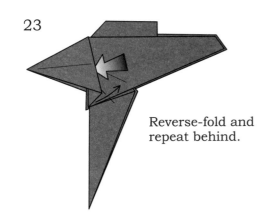

Reverse-fold and repeat behind.

24

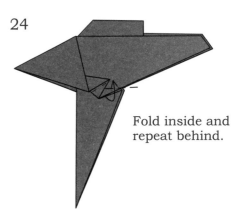

Fold inside and repeat behind.

25

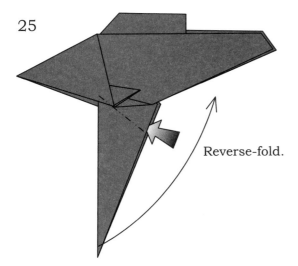

Reverse-fold.

26

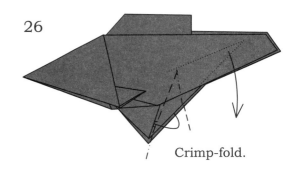

Crimp-fold.

27

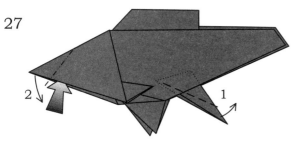

1. Outside-reverse-fold.
2. Reverse-fold.

28

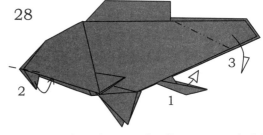

1. Spread and open the fin. Repeat behind.
2. Fold the layers together.
3. Repeat behind.

29

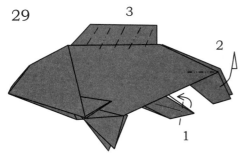

1. Reverse-fold.
2. Fold one layer up.
3. Pleat the fins.

30

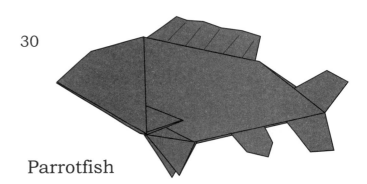

Parrotfish

Ocean Sunfish

Ocean sunfishes (*Mola molas*) live in the open seas in temperate and tropical areas. They can grow to 13 feet and weigh 600 pounds. The young swim in a vertical position while adults often swim on their side. They feed on plankton, fish, and crustaceans.

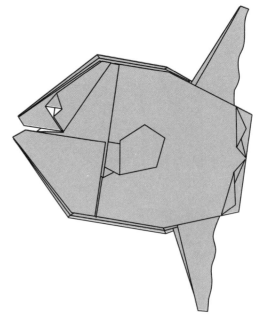

1

Fold and unfold.

2

Fold and unfold.

3

Collapse along the creases.

4

A 3D intermediate step.

5

Squash-fold, repeat behind.

6

Unfold, repeat behind.

7

Fold up and unfold.

8

Bring the dot to the line.

9

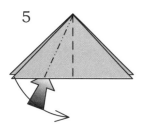

10

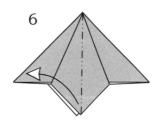

Unfold.

11

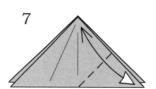

Sink.

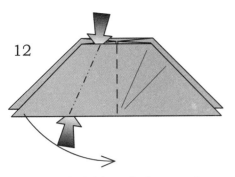

12

Squash-fold again but work
out the top. Repeat behind.

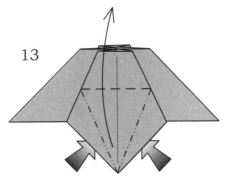

13

Petal-fold. Repeat behind.

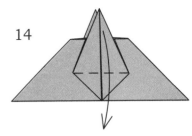

14

Repeat behind and rotate.

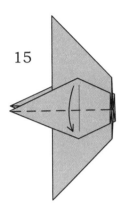

15

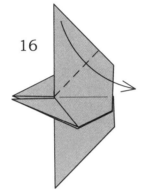

16

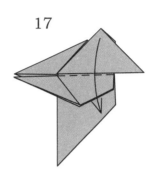

17

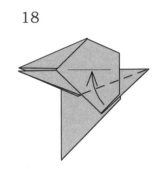

18

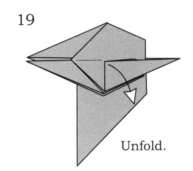

19

Unfold.

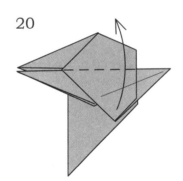

20

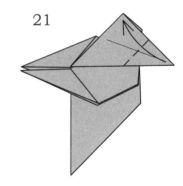

21

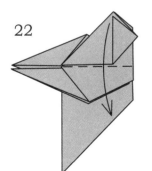

22

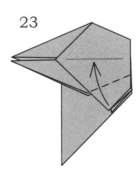

23

Lift the top layers up
while folding the
hidden fin in half.

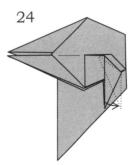

24

Slide to the dotted lines.
The side will be vertical.

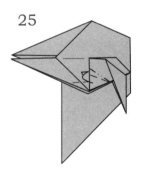

25

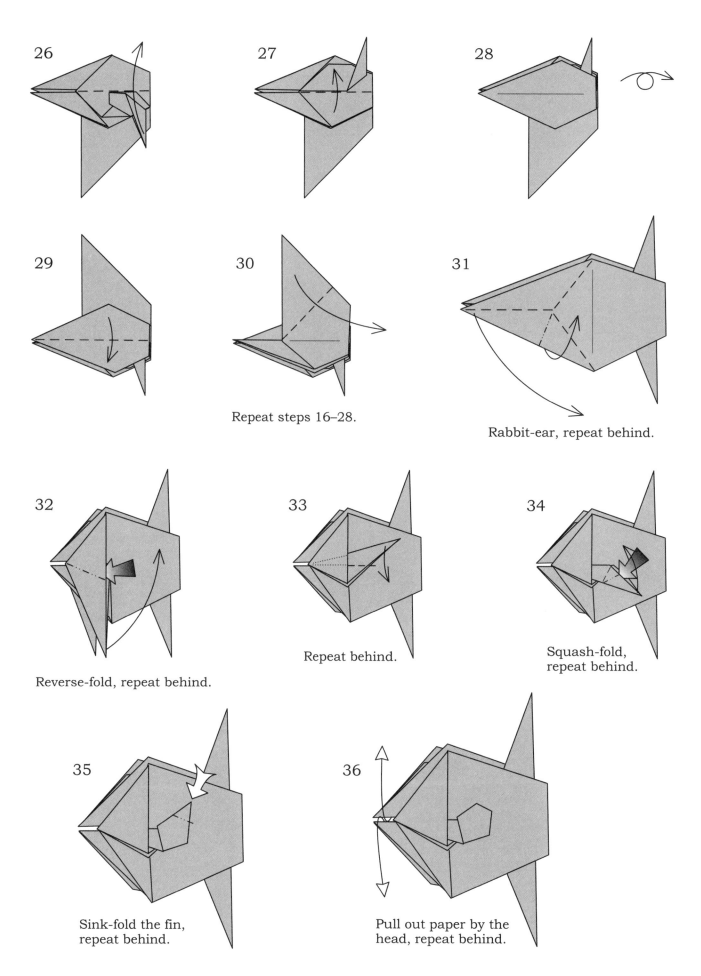

26

27

28

29

30

Repeat steps 16–28.

31

Rabbit-ear, repeat behind.

32

Reverse-fold, repeat behind.

33

Repeat behind.

34

Squash-fold, repeat behind.

35

Sink-fold the fin, repeat behind.

36

Pull out paper by the head, repeat behind.

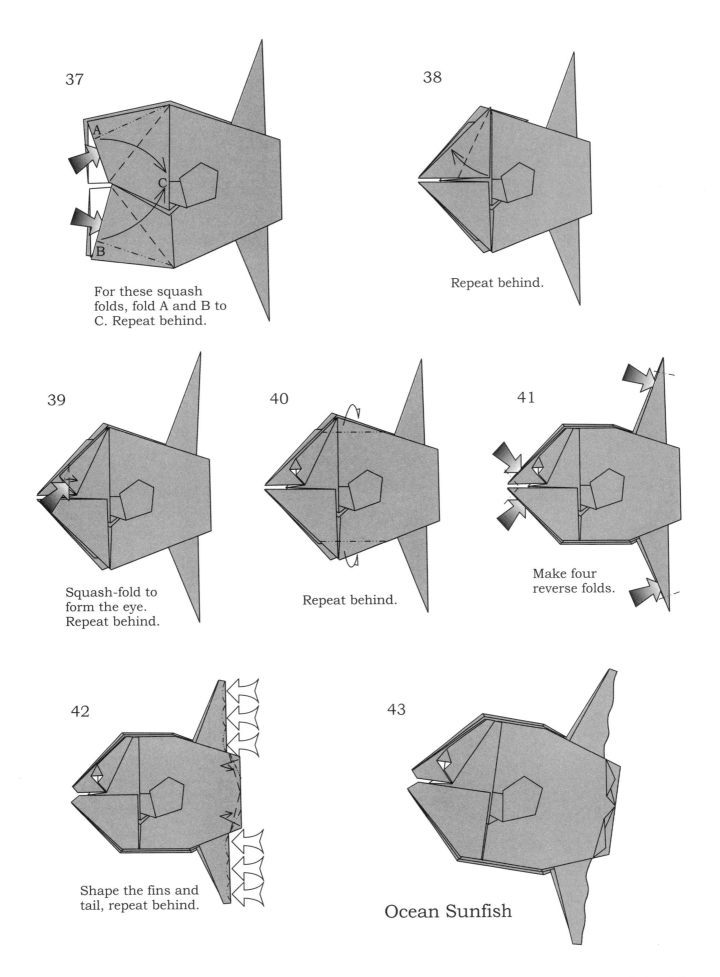

37

For these squash folds, fold A and B to C. Repeat behind.

38

Repeat behind.

39

Squash-fold to form the eye. Repeat behind.

40

Repeat behind.

41

Make four reverse folds.

42

Shape the fins and tail, repeat behind.

43

Ocean Sunfish

Triggerfish

It is quite easy to tell where the triggerfish (*Balistes*) gets its name—the first three dorsal spines are thick and robust and resemble a trigger in shape. This apparatus is locked into place while the fish wedges itself into a crevice, making it almost impossible to extract, a very effective defense mechanism. These fish are found on tropical reefs world wide and are spectacularly colored. Their favorite food is sea urchin. Large specimens may reach a foot in length.

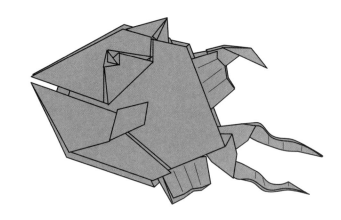

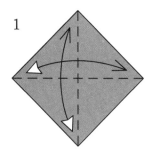

1

Fold and unfold.

2

Fold and unfold.

3

Collapse along the creases.

4

Kite fold,
repeat behind.

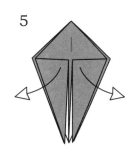

5

Unfold, repeat behind.

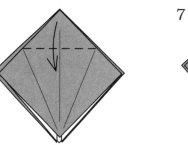

6

7

Unfold.

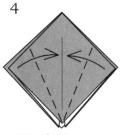

8

Sink.

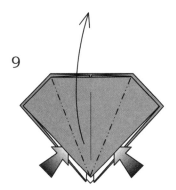

9

Petal-fold,
repeat behind.

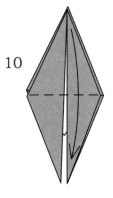

10

Repeat behind.

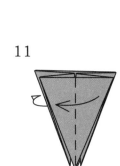

11

Rotate.

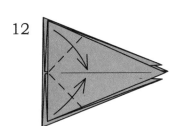

12

Repeat behind.

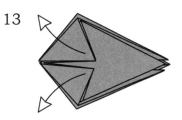

13

Unfold, repeat behind.

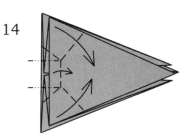

14

Repeat behind.

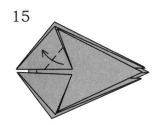

15

Repeat behind.

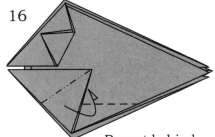

16

Repeat behind.

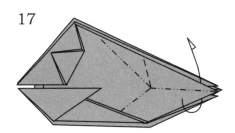

17

Rabbit-ear.
Repeat behind.

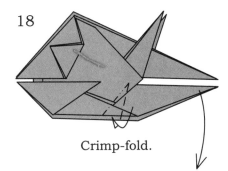

18

Crimp-fold.

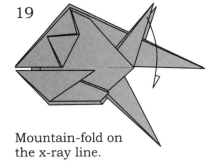

19

Mountain-fold on
the x-ray line.

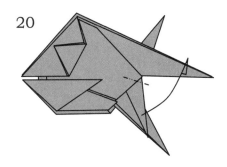

20

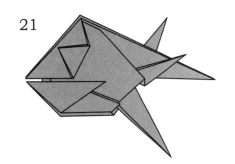

21

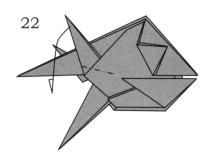

22

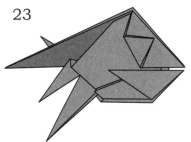

23

An x-ray view of the darker flap will be shown in the next step.

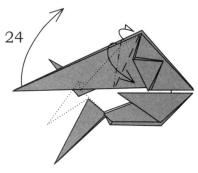

24

Crimp-fold the long flap. Some of the outer paper is drawn with dotted lines so the inner layer can be seen.

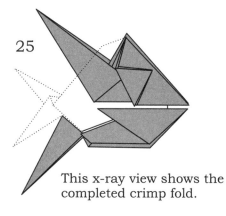

25

This x-ray view shows the completed crimp fold.

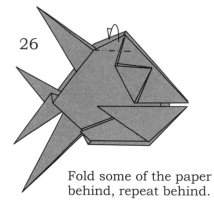

26

Fold some of the paper behind, repeat behind.

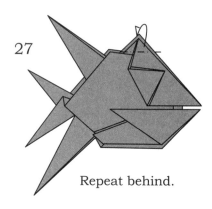

27

Repeat behind.

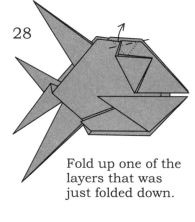

28

Fold up one of the layers that was just folded down.

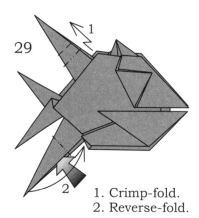

29

1. Crimp-fold.
2. Reverse-fold.

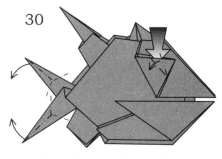

30

Double-rabbit-ear the tips of the tail. Squash-fold the eyes. Repeat behind.

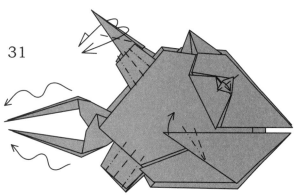

31

Repeat behind.

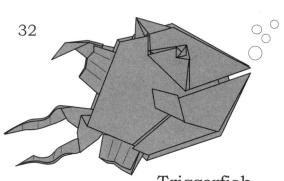

32

Triggerfish

Cichlid

This family of fishes (family *Cichlidae*) is extremely diverse. One group of cichlids (pronounced "SIK-lids") looks like a freshwater barracuda, while another is flat and disc shaped. They are small to medium in size and of all colors. They eat small marine animals. Many are found throughout Central and South America and Africa.

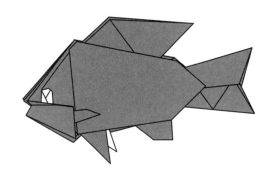

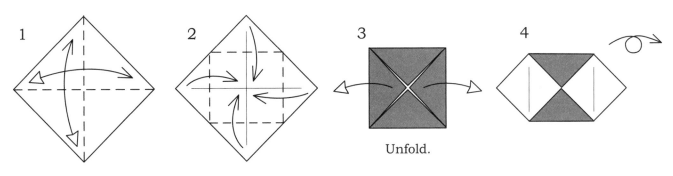

1

Fold and unfold.

2

3

Unfold.

4

5

6

Unfold.

7

8

Unfold.

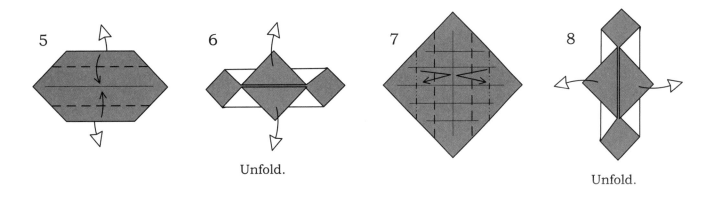

9

Fold and unfold.

10

11

12

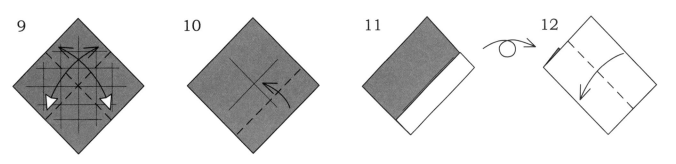

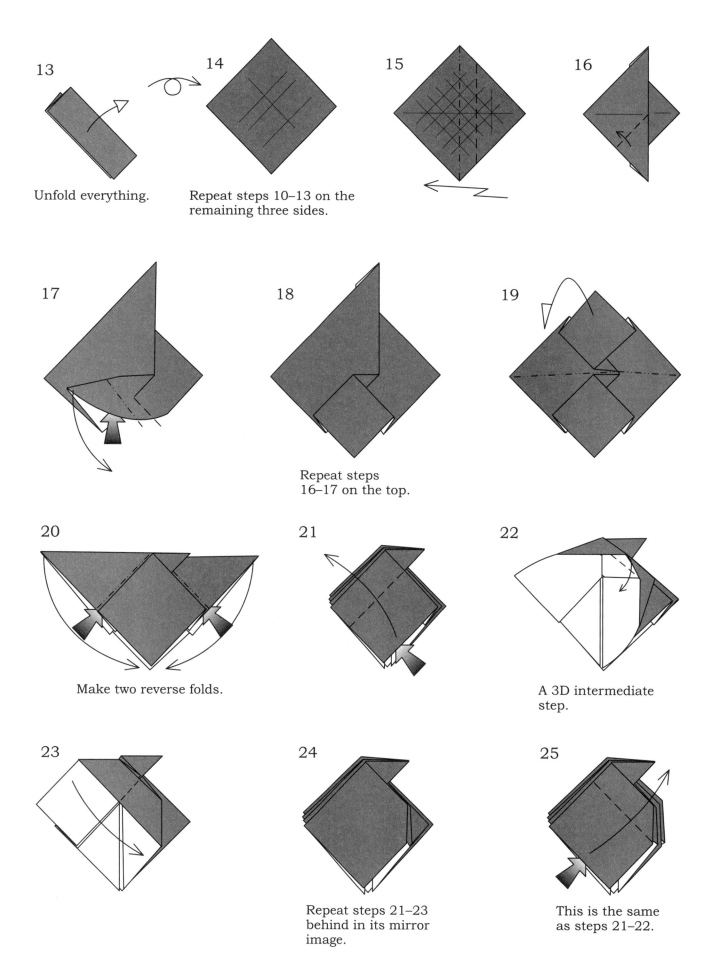

13

Unfold everything.

14

Repeat steps 10–13 on the remaining three sides.

15

16

17

18

Repeat steps 16–17 on the top.

19

20

Make two reverse folds.

21

22

A 3D intermediate step.

23

24

Repeat steps 21–23 behind in its mirror image.

25

This is the same as steps 21–22.

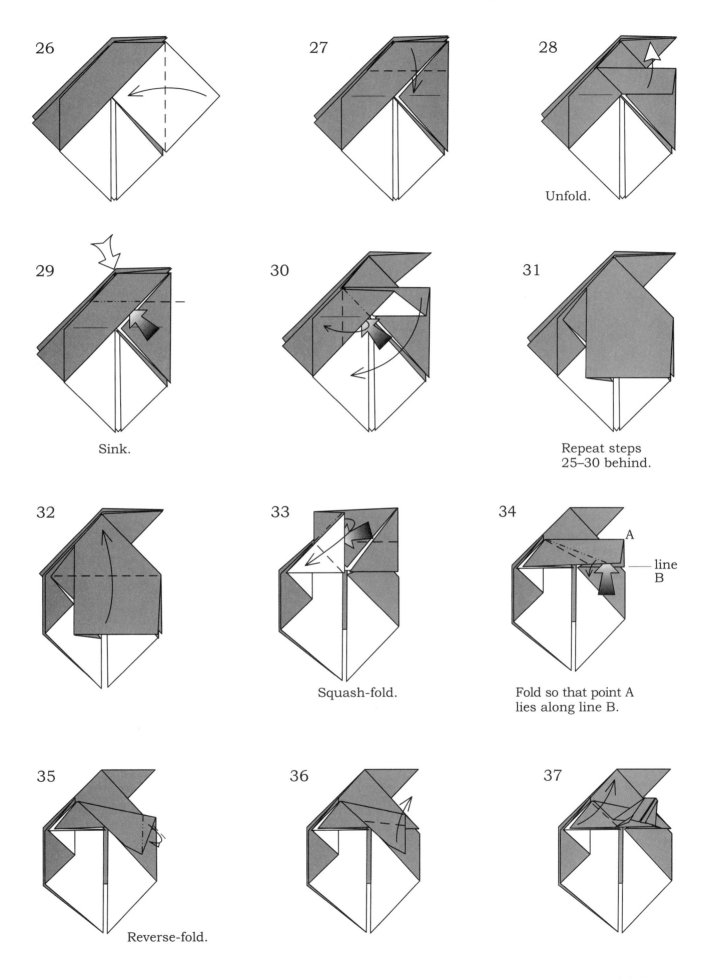

26

27

28

Unfold.

29

Sink.

30

31

Repeat steps
25–30 behind.

32

33

Squash-fold.

34

A

line
B

Fold so that point A
lies along line B.

35

Reverse-fold.

36

37

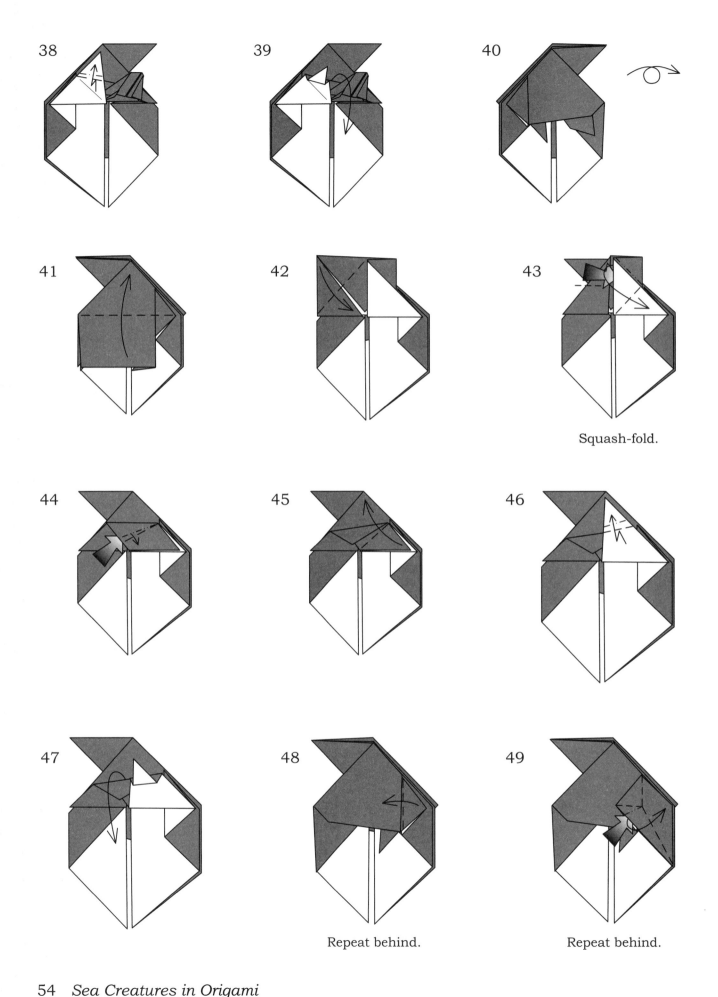

43 Squash-fold.

48 Repeat behind.

49 Repeat behind.

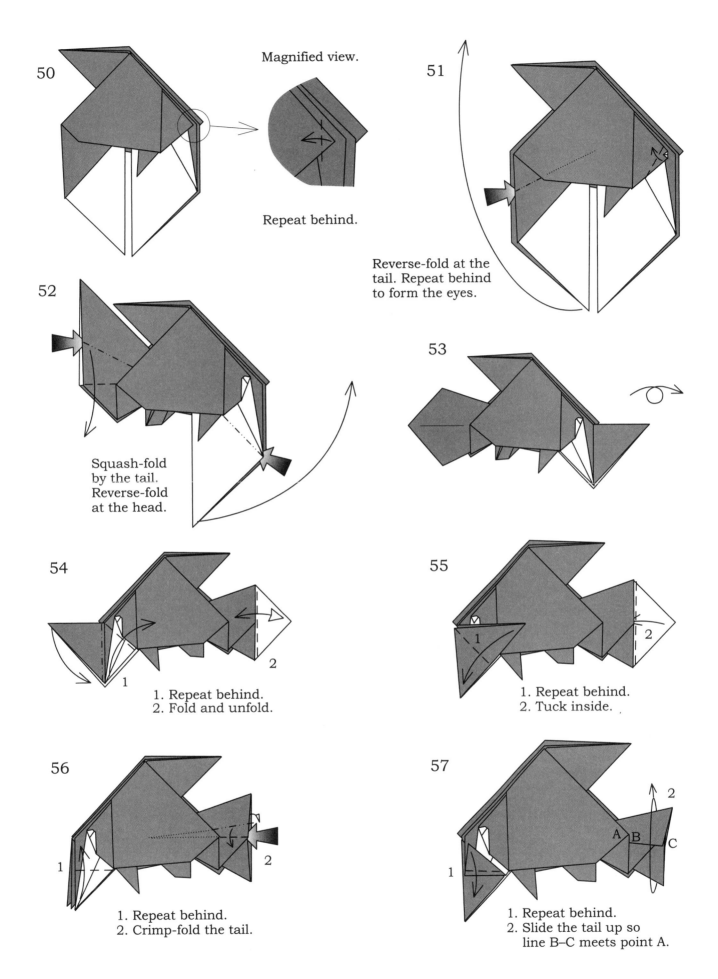

50

Magnified view.

Repeat behind.

51

Reverse-fold at the
tail. Repeat behind
to form the eyes.

52

Squash-fold
by the tail.
Reverse-fold
at the head.

53

54

1. Repeat behind.
2. Fold and unfold.

55

1. Repeat behind.
2. Tuck inside.

56

1. Repeat behind.
2. Crimp-fold the tail.

57

A B
C

1. Repeat behind.
2. Slide the tail up so
   line B–C meets point A.

58

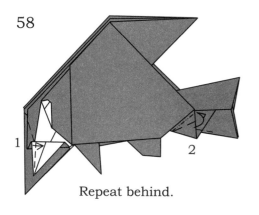

1

2

Repeat behind.

59

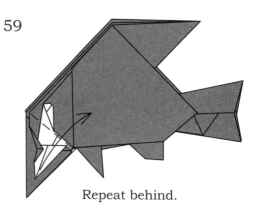

Repeat behind.

60

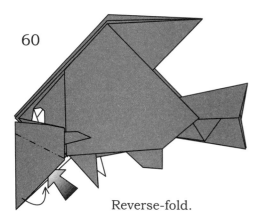

Reverse-fold.

61

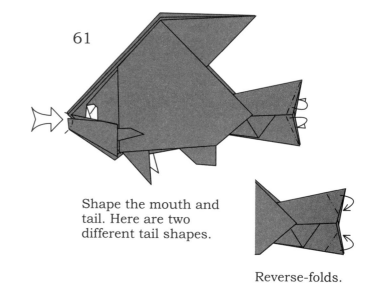

Shape the mouth and tail. Here are two different tail shapes.

Reverse-folds.

62

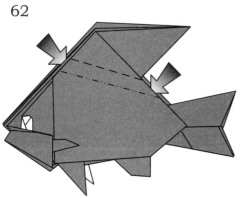

This fold is a cross between the sink and crimp fold. It forms the upper body and dorsal fin. Do this fold slowly. Only one of the two tails is drawn.

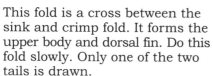

Cichlids

63

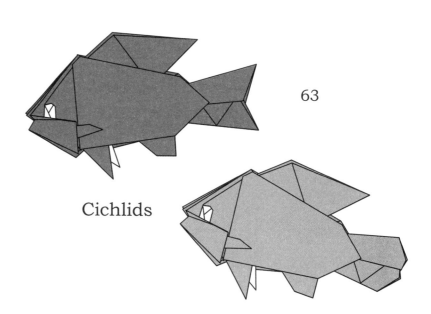

Sailfish

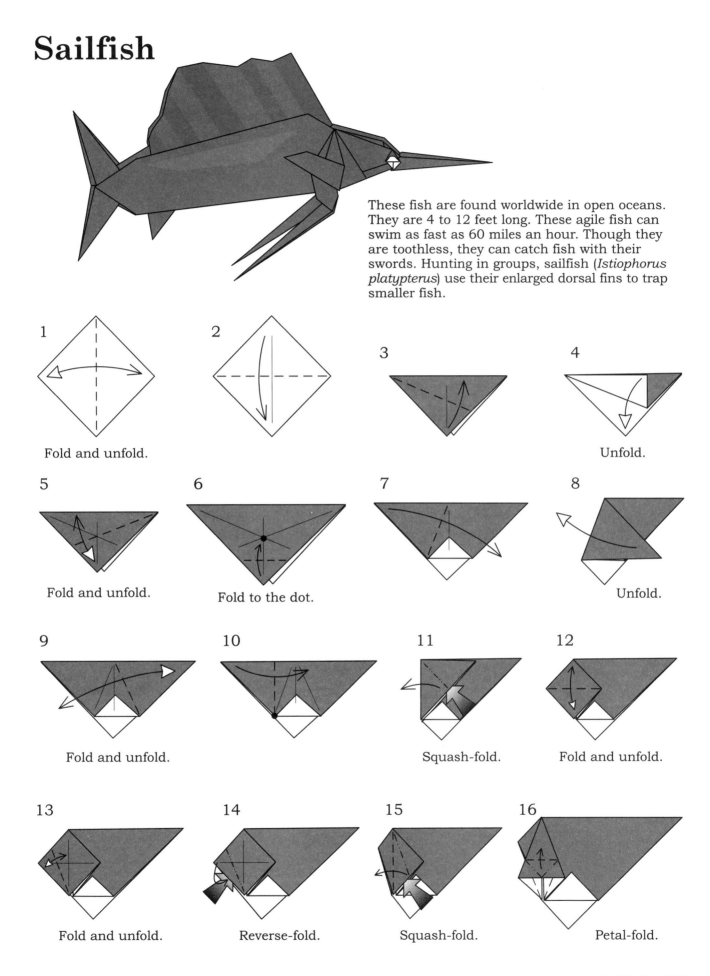

These fish are found worldwide in open oceans. They are 4 to 12 feet long. These agile fish can swim as fast as 60 miles an hour. Though they are toothless, they can catch fish with their swords. Hunting in groups, sailfish (*Istiophorus platypterus*) use their enlarged dorsal fins to trap smaller fish.

1

Fold and unfold.

2

3

4

Unfold.

5

Fold and unfold.

6

Fold to the dot.

7

8

Unfold.

9

Fold and unfold.

10

11

Squash-fold.

12

Fold and unfold.

13

Fold and unfold.

14

Reverse-fold.

15

Squash-fold.

16

Petal-fold.

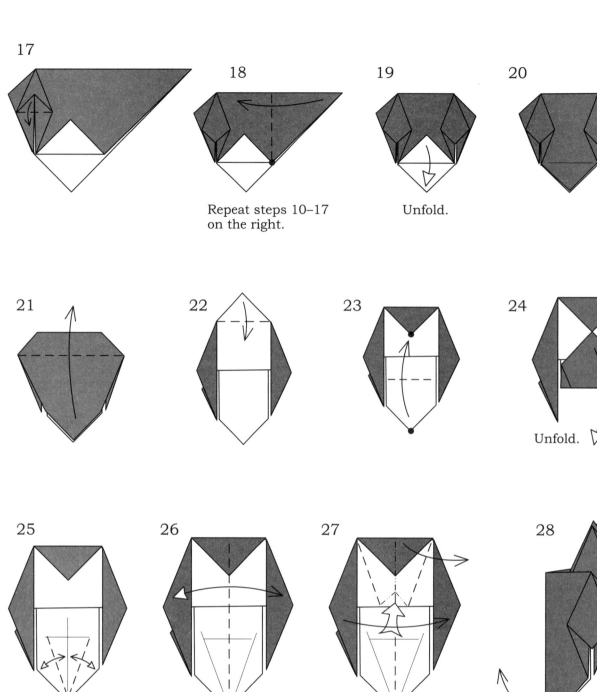

17

18

Repeat steps 10–17
on the right.

19

Unfold.

20

21

22

23

24

Unfold.

25

Fold and unfold.

26

Fold and unfold.

27

Push the center in to
form a little diamond
while folding in half.

28

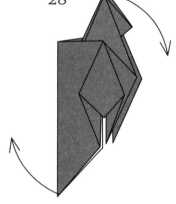

Rotate the model.

29

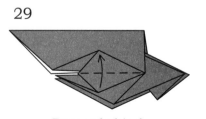

Repeat behind.

30

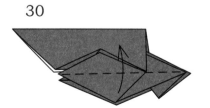

Repeat behind.

31

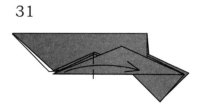

Repeat behind.

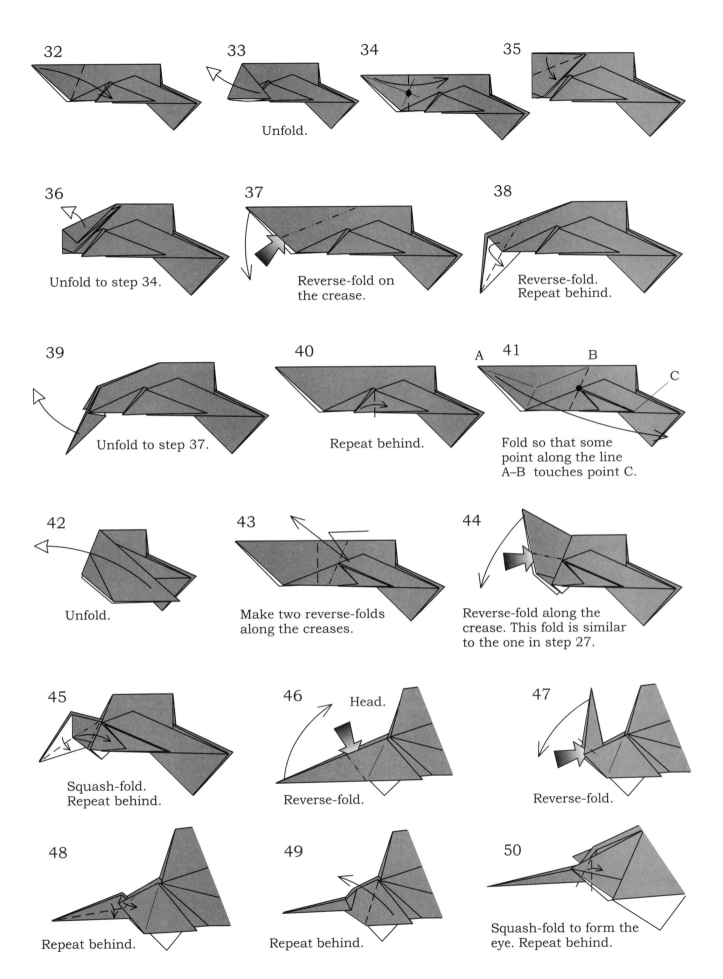

32

33

Unfold.

34

35

36

Unfold to step 34.

37

Reverse-fold on
the crease.

38

Reverse-fold.
Repeat behind.

39

Unfold to step 37.

40

Repeat behind.

A   41   B   C

Fold so that some
point along the line
A–B touches point C.

42

Unfold.

43

Make two reverse-folds
along the creases.

44

Reverse-fold along the
crease. This fold is similar
to the one in step 27.

45

Squash-fold.
Repeat behind.

46

Head.

Reverse-fold.

47

Reverse-fold.

48

Repeat behind.

49

Repeat behind.

50

Squash-fold to form the
eye. Repeat behind.

Sailfish 59

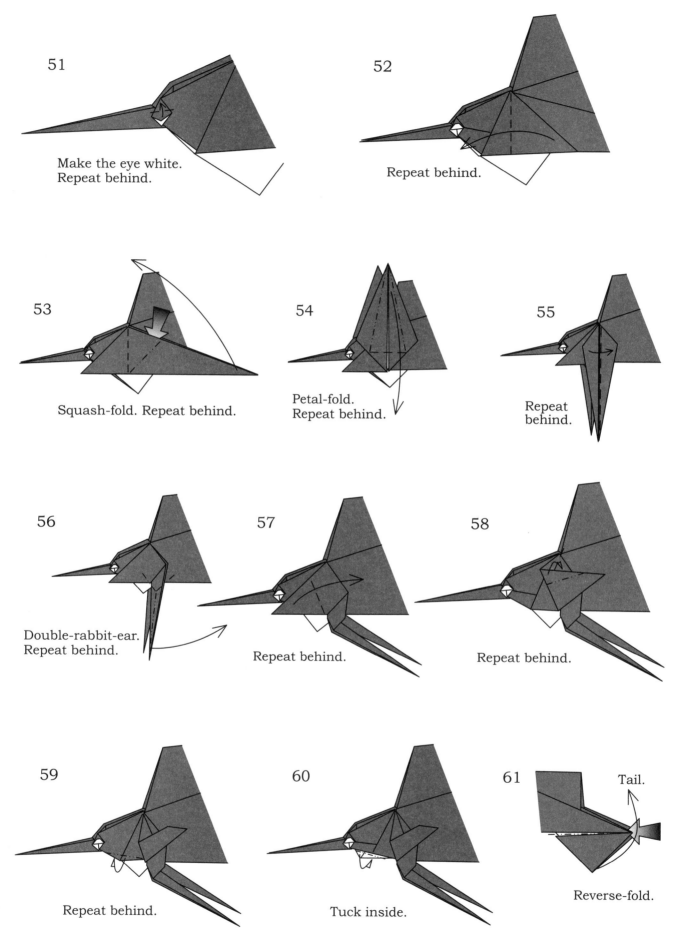

51

Make the eye white.
Repeat behind.

52

Repeat behind.

53

Squash-fold. Repeat behind.

54

Petal-fold.
Repeat behind.

55

Repeat
behind.

56

Double-rabbit-ear.
Repeat behind.

57

Repeat behind.

58

Repeat behind.

59

Repeat behind.

60

Tuck inside.

61

Tail.

Reverse-fold.

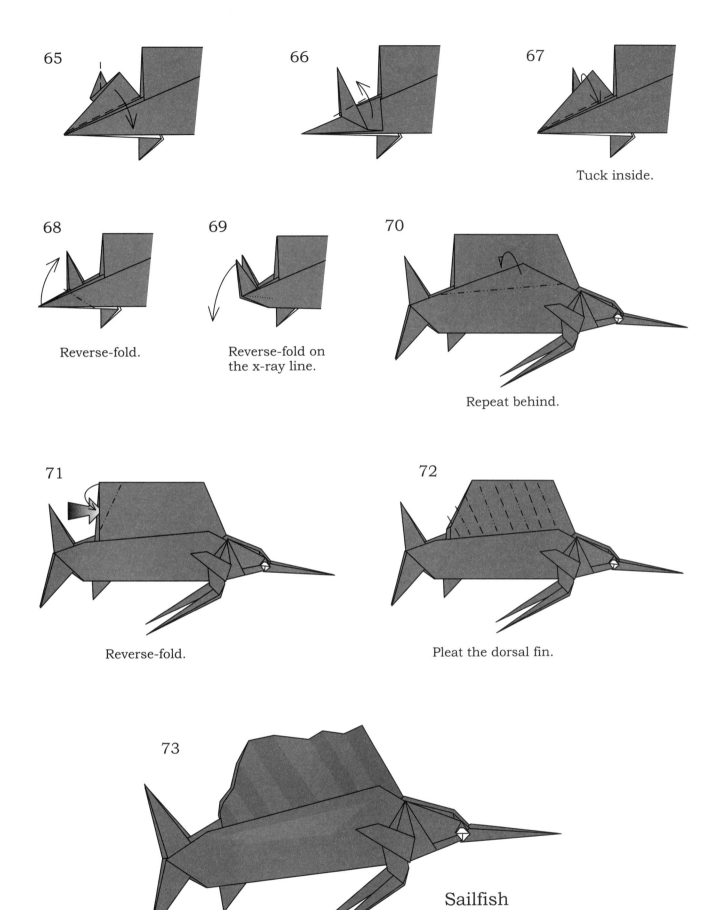

65

66

67

Tuck inside.

68

Reverse-fold.

69

Reverse-fold on
the x-ray line.

70

Repeat behind.

71

Reverse-fold.

72

Pleat the dorsal fin.

73

Sailfish

Blue Shark

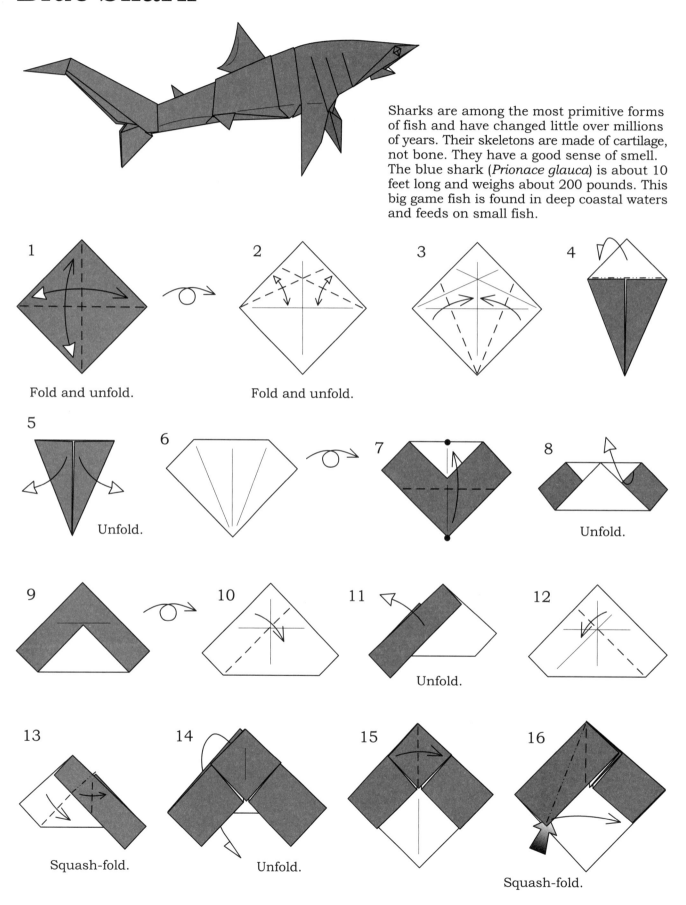

Sharks are among the most primitive forms of fish and have changed little over millions of years. Their skeletons are made of cartilage, not bone. They have a good sense of smell. The blue shark (*Prionace glauca*) is about 10 feet long and weighs about 200 pounds. This big game fish is found in deep coastal waters and feeds on small fish.

1

Fold and unfold.

2

Fold and unfold.

3

4

5

Unfold.

6

7

8

Unfold.

9

10

11

Unfold.

12

13

Squash-fold.

14

Unfold.

15

16

Squash-fold.

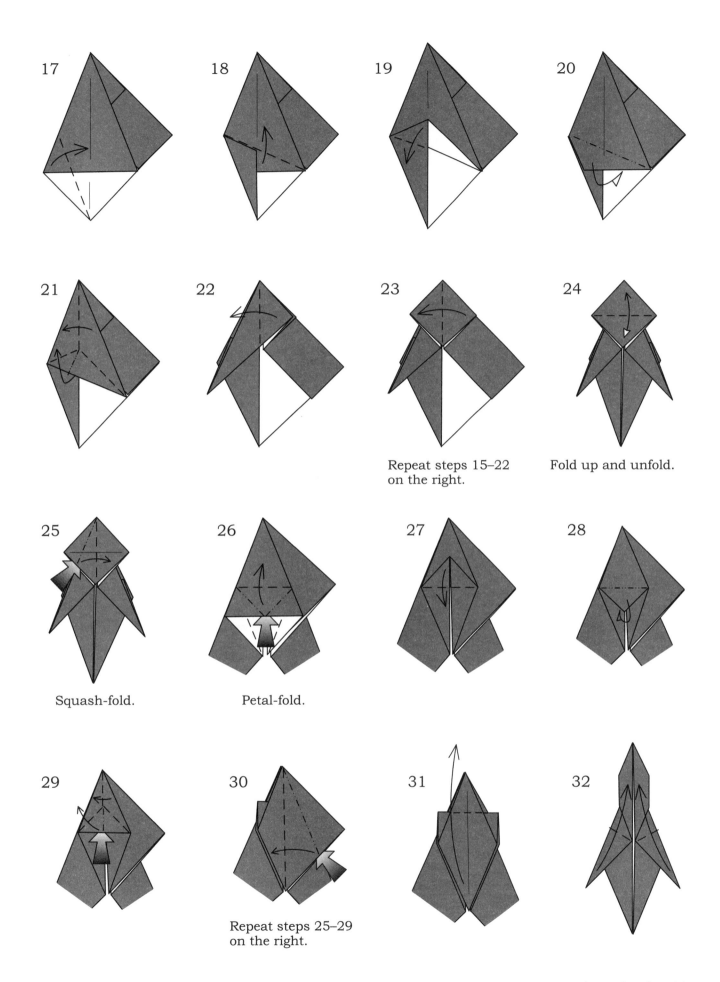

17

18

19

20

21

22

23

Repeat steps 15–22
on the right.

24

Fold up and unfold.

25

Squash-fold.

26

Petal-fold.

27

28

29

30

Repeat steps 25–29
on the right.

31

32

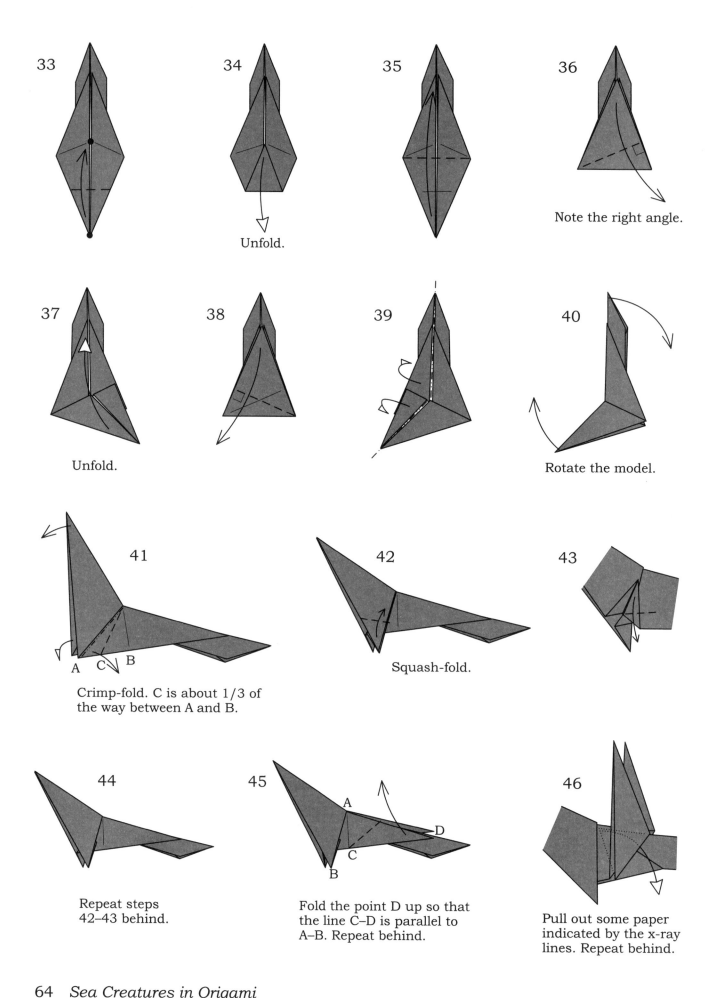

33

34

Unfold.

35

36

Note the right angle.

37

Unfold.

38

39

Rotate the model.

40

41

Crimp-fold. C is about 1/3 of the way between A and B.

A   C   B

42

Squash-fold.

43

44

Repeat steps 42–43 behind.

45

A

D

C

B

Fold the point D up so that the line C–D is parallel to A–B. Repeat behind.

46

Pull out some paper indicated by the x-ray lines. Repeat behind.

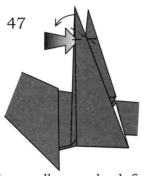

47

The small upper back fin will now be formed. There are no guide lines for this squash fold, but do not make it too small.

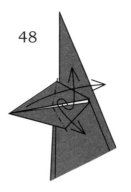

48

Spread the paper while folding to the right.

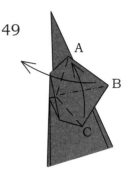

49

Fold C to A while B is folded up and to the left.

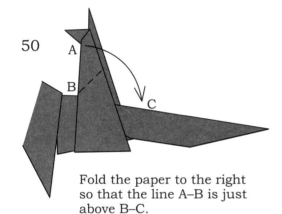

50

Fold the paper to the right so that the line A–B is just above B–C.

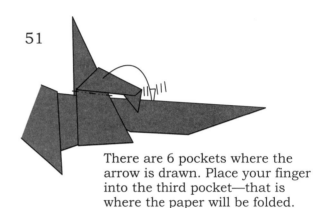

51

There are 6 pockets where the arrow is drawn. Place your finger into the third pocket—that is where the paper will be folded.

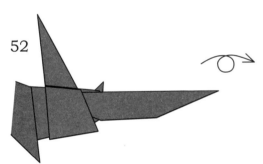

52

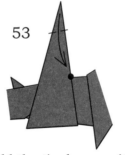

53

Fold the tip down so it is a bit above the dot.

54

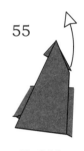

55

Unfold.

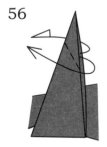

56

Outside-reverse-fold along the creases.

57

Pull out some paper. Repeat behind.

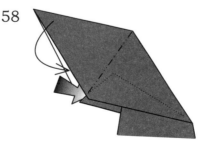

58

Reverse-fold the tip into the layer shown by the x-ray lines and large arrow. This will lock the fin.

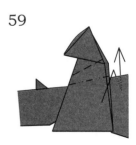

59

Pleat-fold to place the fin. Some of the paper is folded into the third layer. Give this fold a good, sharp crease.

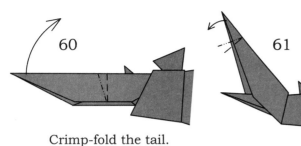

60

Crimp-fold the tail.

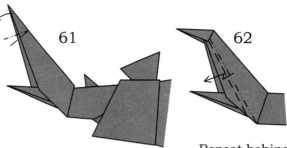

61

Crimp-fold the
tip of the tail.

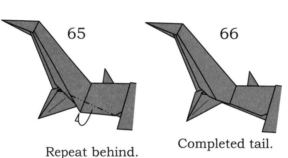

62

Repeat behind.

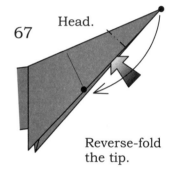

63

Place your finger into
the most central layer
to reverse-fold the
lower part of the tail.

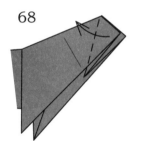

64

Pull out two layers to widen
the tail. The dotted lines
show where the paper will
go. Repeat behind.

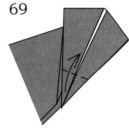

65

Repeat behind.

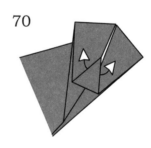
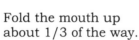

66

Completed tail.

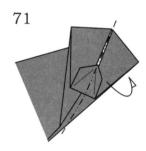

67

Head.

Reverse-fold
the tip.

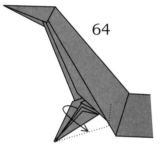

68

69

Fold the mouth up
about 1/3 of the way.

70

Spread the paper to
form the mouth.

71

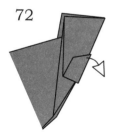

72

Slide the mouth.

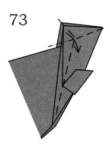

73

Rabbit-ear.
Repeat behind.

74

Step 75 shows an
enlarged view.

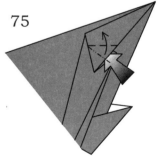

75

Squash-fold to form the
eye. Repeat behind.

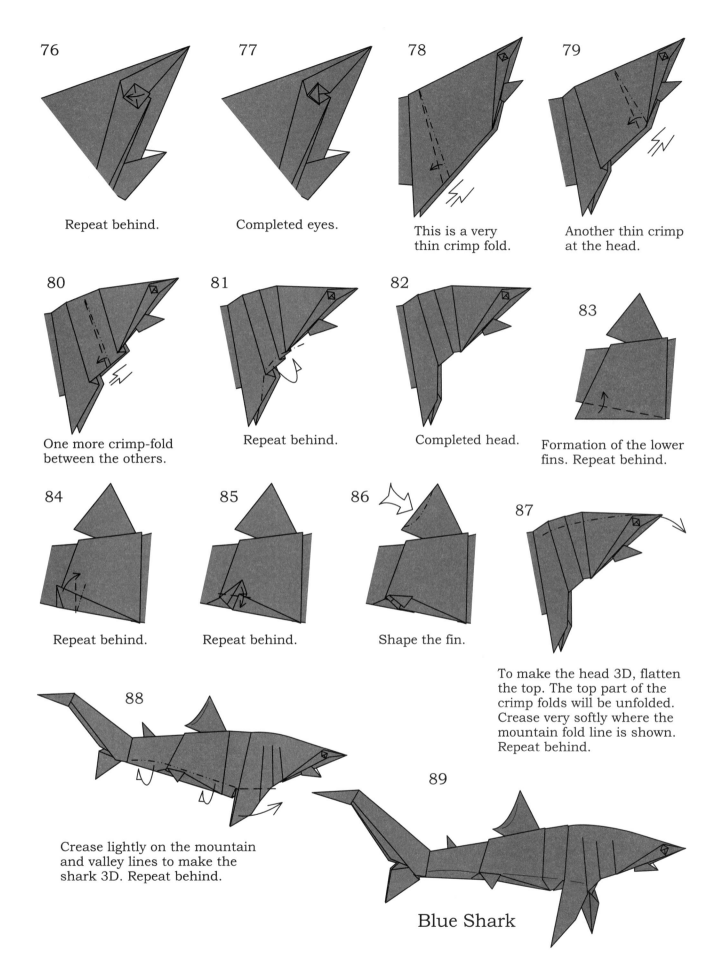

76

Repeat behind.

77

Completed eyes.

78

This is a very thin crimp fold.

79

Another thin crimp at the head.

80

One more crimp-fold between the others.

81

Repeat behind.

82

Completed head.

83

Formation of the lower fins. Repeat behind.

84

Repeat behind.

85

Repeat behind.

86

Shape the fin.

87

To make the head 3D, flatten the top. The top part of the crimp folds will be unfolded. Crease very softly where the mountain fold line is shown. Repeat behind.

88

Crease lightly on the mountain and valley lines to make the shark 3D. Repeat behind.

89

Blue Shark

Blackdevil Angler

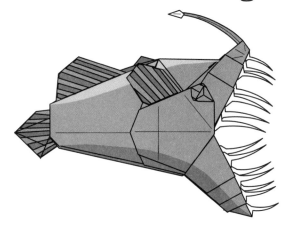

The Blackdevil Angler (*Melanocetus niger*) may well be one of the most scary fishes in the world. But despite their ferocious appearance, deep sea anglers rarely reach six inches in length. They are black and tend to have warty growths over their body. The female is much larger than the male, which lives its life parasitically attached to the female's body. This greatly enhances the chances for reproduction in an environment where individuals might otherwise never meet another of their own species.

1

Crease. Turn
the paper over.

2

Crease the
diagonals.

3

Fold the corners
behind.

4

Fold a hybrid
Waterbomb Base/
Preliminary Fold.

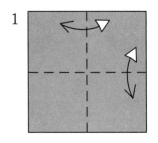

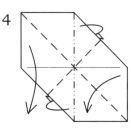

5

Squash-fold. Repeat behind.

6

Fold one layer to the
right in front and one
to the left in back.

7

Squash-fold.
Repeat behind.

8

Petal-fold.
Repeat behind.

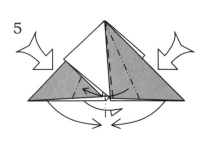

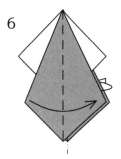

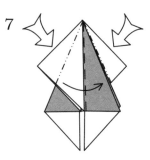

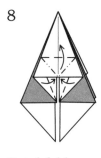

9

Unwrap the trapped
layer of paper.
Repeat behind.

10

Squash-fold.
Repeat behind.

11

Squash-fold.

12

Petal-fold.

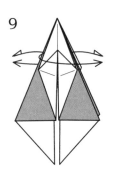

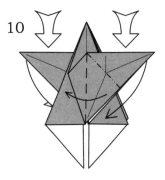

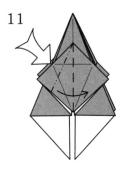

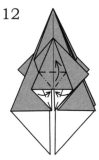

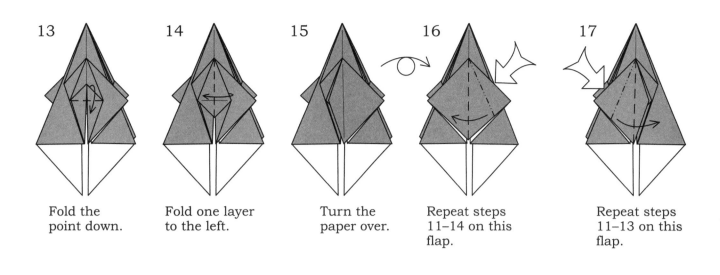

13 Fold the point down.

14 Fold one layer to the left.

15 Turn the paper over.

16 Repeat steps 11–14 on this flap.

17 Repeat steps 11–13 on this flap.

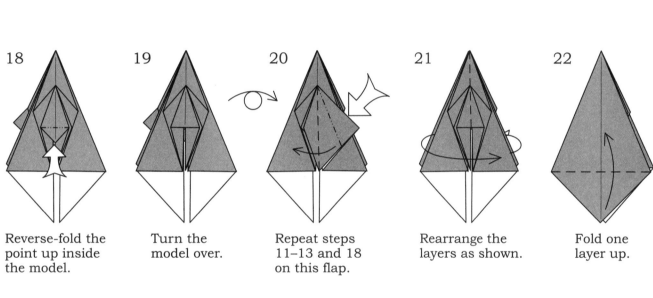

18 Reverse-fold the point up inside the model.

19 Turn the model over.

20 Repeat steps 11–13 and 18 on this flap.

21 Rearrange the layers as shown.

22 Fold one layer up.

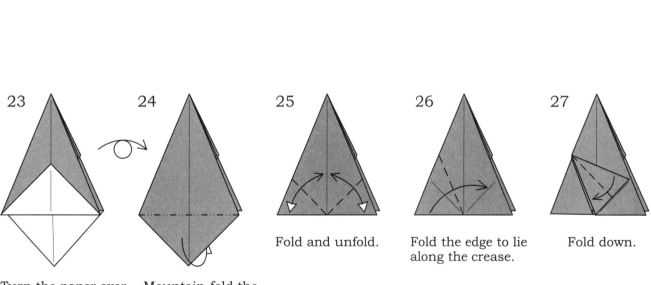

23 Turn the paper over.

24 Mountain-fold the point up into the inside of the model.

25 Fold and unfold.

26 Fold the edge to lie along the crease.

27 Fold down.

28

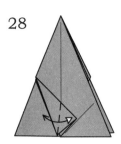

Fold and unfold.

29

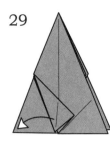

Unfold.

30

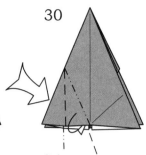

Crimp symmetrically.

31

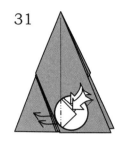

Reverse-fold both corners back to the outside on existing creases.

32

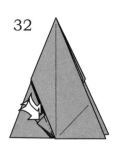

Reverse-fold both corners.

33

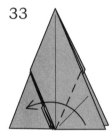

Repeat steps 26–32 on the right.

34

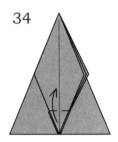

Fold one point up as far as possible.

35

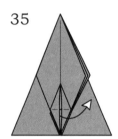

Pull the trapped layers of paper entirely out.

36

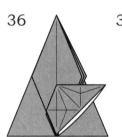

Like this.

37

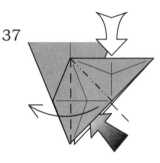

Enlarged view. Squash-fold the flap.

38

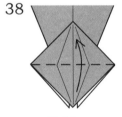

Fold one layer up.

39

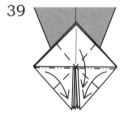

Form a Preliminary Fold.

40

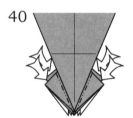

Reverse-fold four corners.

41

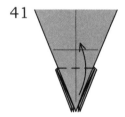

Fold one point up as far as possible.

42

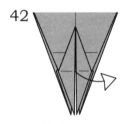

Pull the trapped layer out from the interior.

43

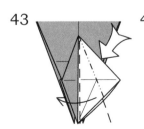

Squash-fold.

44

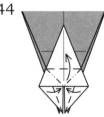

Petal-fold.

45

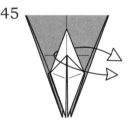

Unwrap the loose layer of paper.

46

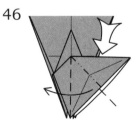

Squash-fold.

47

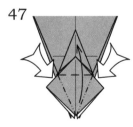

Petal-fold.

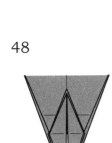

48

Like this.

49

Enlarged view of the tip. Fold the tip down so that the crease lines up with the edge underneath.

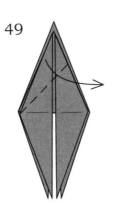

50

Unfold.

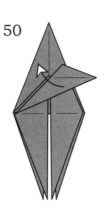

51

Fold and unfold.

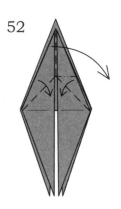

52

Rabbit-ear the flap using the creases you just made.

53

Wrap one layer of paper from inside to the outside.

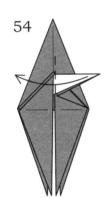

54

Fold the point over to the left.

55

Repeat step 53.

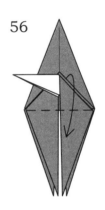

56

Fold all layers downward.

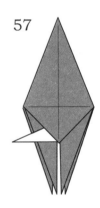

57

Like this.

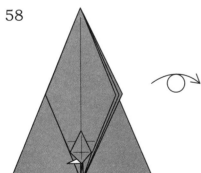

58

This is the entire model. Turn the paper over.

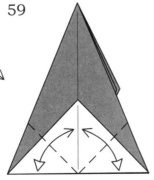

59

Repeat steps 25–33 on this side.

60

Pull out the loose paper.

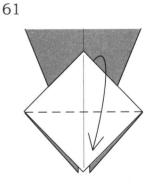

61

Fold one layer down.

62

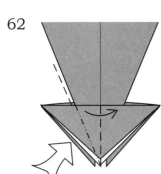

Squash-fold.

63

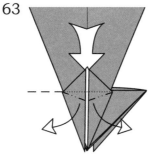

Squash-fold
again.

64

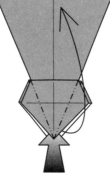

Close up, incorpor-
ating the reverse
fold shown.

65

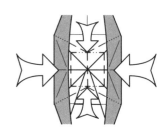

Repeat steps
62–64 on this
side.

66

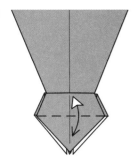

Fold and unfold
the top.

67

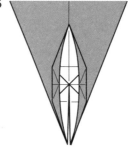

Grasp a single layer
and pull it as far
upward as you can.

68

A white pyramid
forms between the
colored layers.

69

Enlarged view.
Collapse the pyramid
on the creases shown.

70

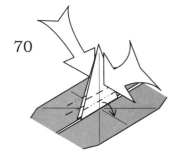

Crimp it
symmetrically
downward.

71

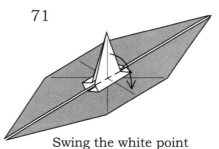

Swing the white point
over to one side.

72

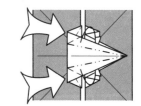

Enlarged view. Swivel-
fold the edges inside.

73

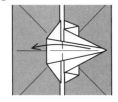

Fold the point back
to the left.

74

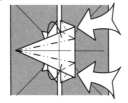

Repeat step 72
on this side.

75

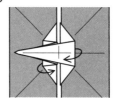

Tuck the edges under
the colored layers.

76

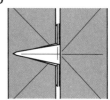

Like this.

77

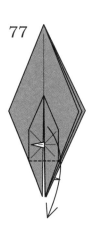

Fold the point downward.

78

Fold the edges in to the center.

79

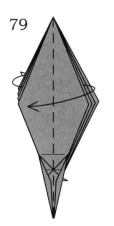

Fold two layers to the left in front and two to the right behind.

80

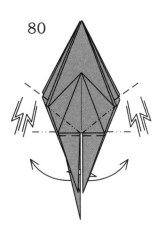

Crimp symmetrically through all layers.

81

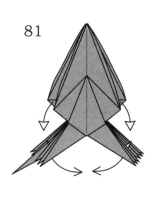

Undo the crimps.

82

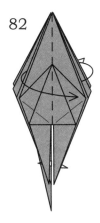

Return the paper to the configuration of step 79.

83

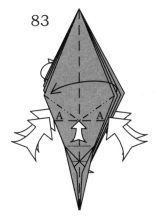

Refold the crimps of step 80 with this change; on the top and bottom single layers of paper, change valley folds to mountain folds and vice-versa. The effect is to sink the edges marked A into themselves (similarly behind).

84

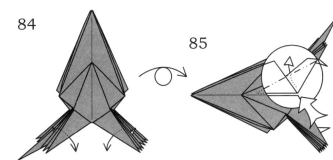

Swing the two white points (the results of steps 57 and 76) downward. Turn the paper over.

85

Sink the inside corner upward as far as possible.

86

Like this.

87

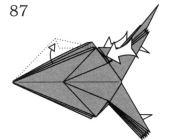

Pull out as much paper as possible; crimps at the white arrows disappear in the process.

88

Like this. X-ray lines show hidden edges.

89

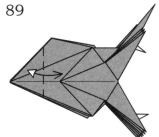

Fold and unfold (there's no reference point).

90

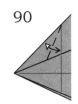

Enlarged view of tail. Crease the angle bisector.

91

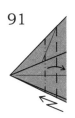

Pleat through all layers.

92

Swivel-fold.

93

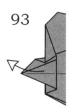

Unfold to step 90.

94

Spread the bottom layers symmetrically to form a three-sided pyramid.

95

Carefully collapse the pyramid on the creases shown.

96

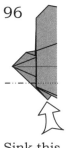

Sink this corner.

97

Swivel-fold the hidden corner.

98

Repeat behind.

99

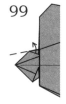

Fold upwards.

100

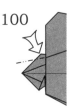

Sink.

101

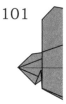

Like this.

102

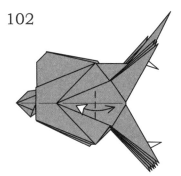

Crease lightly.

103

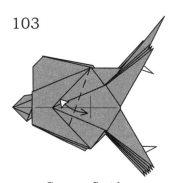

Crease firmly.

104

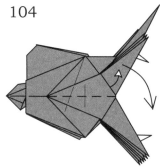

Swing one flap downward, releasing the layers of paper at the crimp.

105

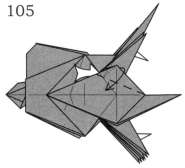

Valley-fold the flap and squash-fold the tiny gusset inside.

106

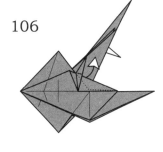

The body and tail are not shown for the next 11 steps. Pull out a single layer of paper.

107

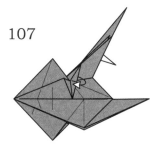

Pull out the layers from under the gusset.

108

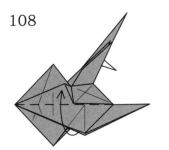

Fold one layer
upward.

109

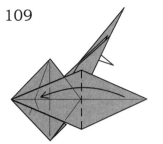

Fold the point
over to the left.

110

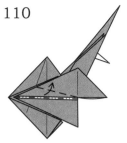

Pleat the top portion of
the point; the bottom
will not lie flat.

111

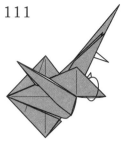

With the pleat in place,
wrap one layer of paper
from front to back.

112

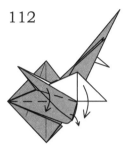

Close the model
up, adding a
second pleat.

113

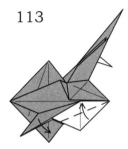

Shift the point slightly
downward and fold the
white edge upward.

114

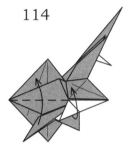

Close up the flap.

115

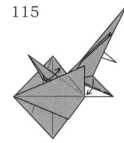

Open out the colored
point and fold the single
layer over the white point.

116

Sink the tip. This
will be a fin.

117

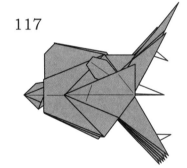

Repeat steps 102–116 on the
other side of the model.

118

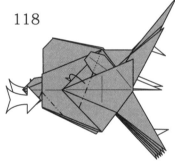

Reverse-fold the corner at the base
of the tail. Mountain-fold the flap
next to the fin. Repeat behind.

119

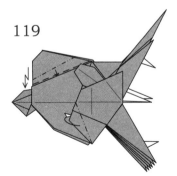

Pleat the top of the model and
tuck it into the pocket shown.
Mountain-fold the bottom of the
model. Repeat behind.

120

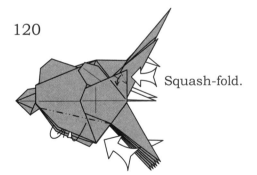

Squash-fold.

Reverse-fold a single layer.

121

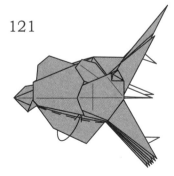

Tuck the remaining layers into
the pocket you just made.

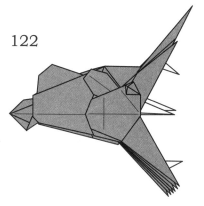

122

Like this.

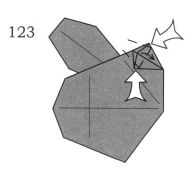

123

Enlarged view of fin and eye.
Petal-fold. Repeat behind.

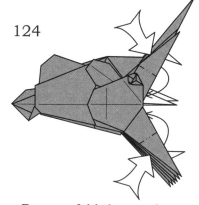

124

Reverse-fold the two front
points into the model.

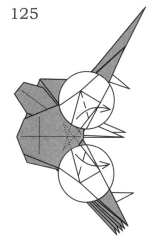

125

Enlarged view of head.
Valley-fold the two
points outward.

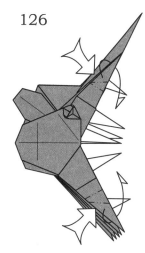

126

Repeat steps 124–125
on the next pair of
points.

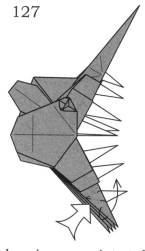

127

And again on a point at the
bottom. Then repeat on all
the points on the other side.

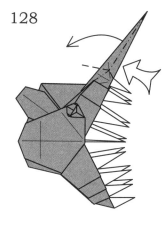

128

Double-rabbit-ear the
long point at the top.

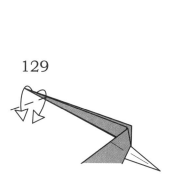

129

Enlarged view. Open out
the layers at the tip.

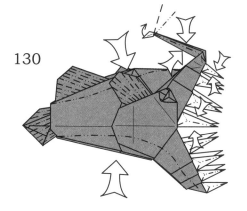

130

Final shaping. Round the body. Pleat
the fins. Pinch the lure and each of the
teeth. Curve the teeth slightly.

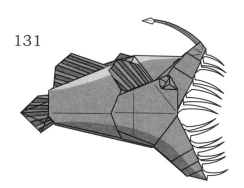

131

Blackdevil Angler

Starfish

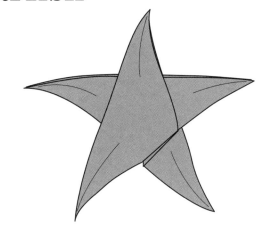

These echinoderms usually have five arms. A newly hatched starfish swims around, settling after awhile to the bottom of the sea. It crawls around the sea floor using its tube feet. The mouth is on the underside of its body and the starfish turns its stomach inside out through the mouth to eat its prey. It feeds on oysters, clams, sponges, and other small animals. When cut, the starfish (*Asterias forbesi*) can grow new arms.

1

Fold and unfold.

2

Make a small crease.

3

Fold the top corner to the center and unfold. Make a small crease.

4

Fold up so the edge meets the dot.

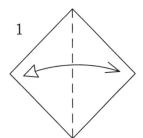 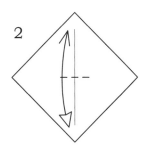 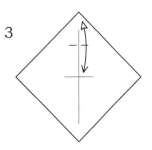 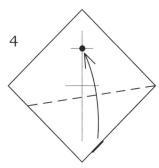

5

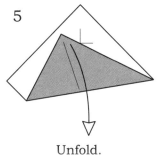

Unfold.

6

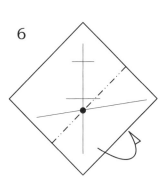

Fold behind using the intersection as a guide.

7

Fold along the hidden edge.

8

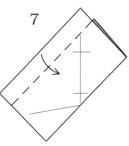 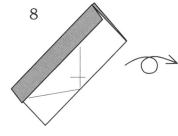

9

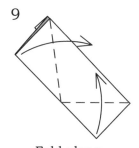

Fold along the creases.

10

11

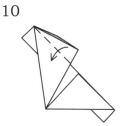 

Unfold almost everything.

12

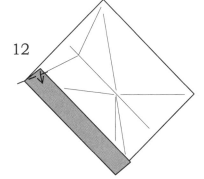

Starfish 77

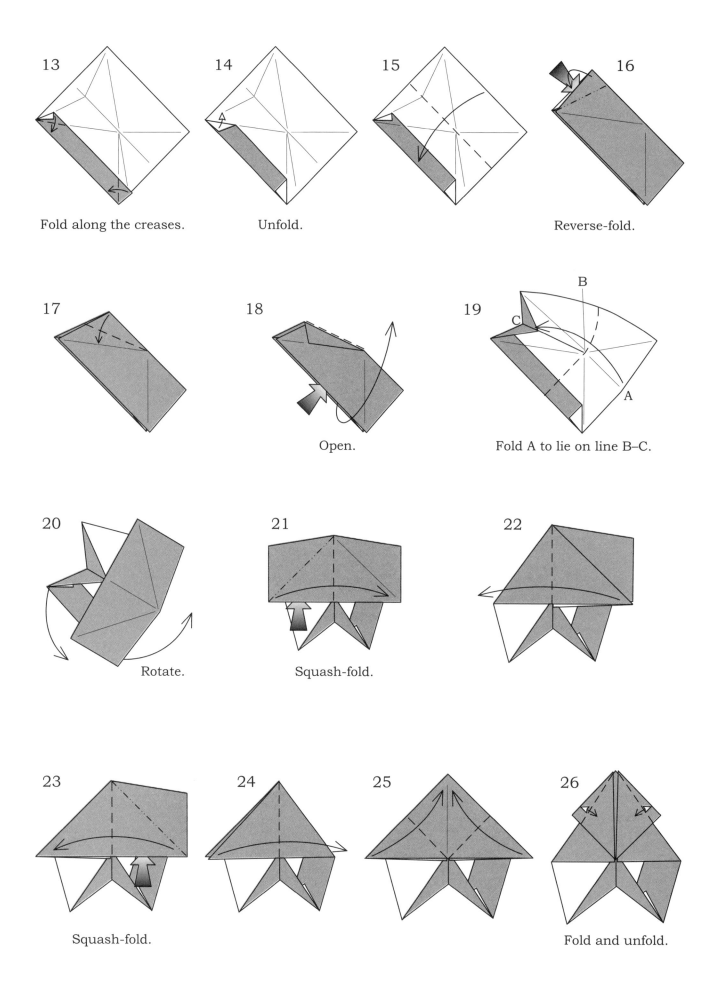

13
Fold along the creases.

14
Unfold.

15

16
Reverse-fold.

17

18
Open.

19
Fold A to lie on line B–C.

20
Rotate.

21
Squash-fold.

22

23
Squash-fold.

24

25

26
Fold and unfold.

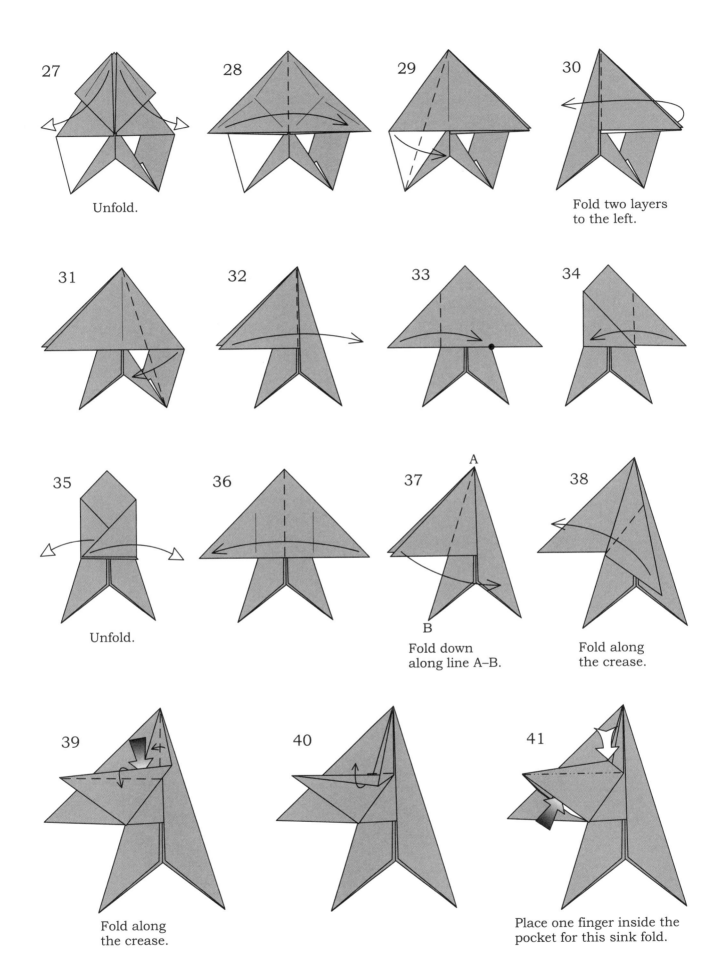

27 Unfold.

28

29

30 Fold two layers to the left.

31

32

33

34

35 Unfold.

36

37 A
B
Fold down along line A–B.

38 Fold along the crease.

39 Fold along the crease.

40

41 Place one finger inside the pocket for this sink fold.

42

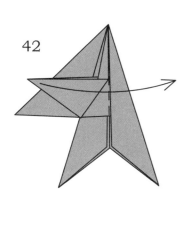

43

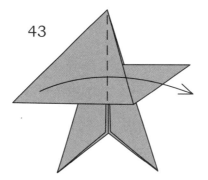

Repeat steps
36–42 on the left.

44

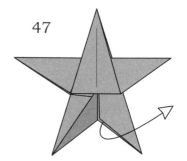

Unfold.

45

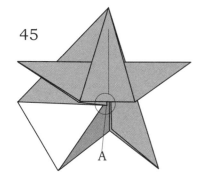

A

Tuck the tiny corner A
under the darker paper.

46

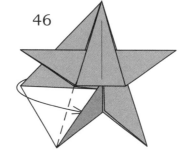

Tuck behind the
darker paper.

47

Repeat steps 44–46
on the right.

48

49

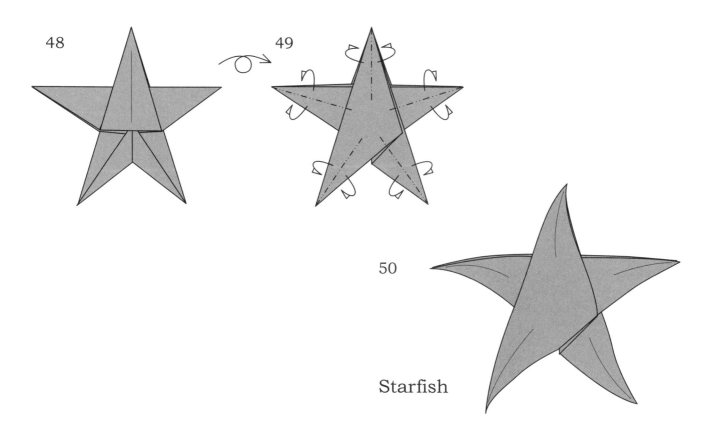

50

Starfish

Sand Dollar

Sand dollars are of the same class as sea urchins, but have shed their spines and adopted a flattened shape suitable for burrowing into sand. They typically stand up vertically in the sand and filter water for plankton. The Keyhole Urchin (*Millita quinquiespertorata*) lives in shallow water below low-tide lines from Cape Cod to the Caribbean and along coastal Mexico and Brazil. Its five slots begin as notches when the animal is young, but close off as it matures.

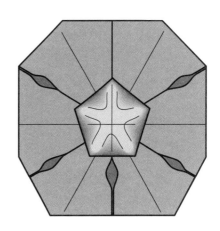

1
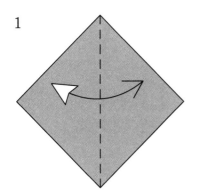

Crease the
vertical diagonal.

2
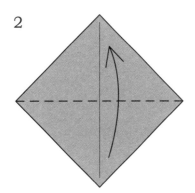

Fold the bottom
corner up to the top.

3
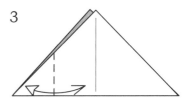

Fold the left corner in to
the middle and unfold.

4
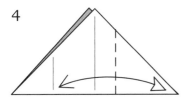

Fold the right corner over
to the crease you just
made and unfold.

5

Fold the left corner up so
that the crease made in
step 3 touches the crease
made in step 4.

6
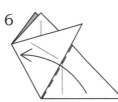

Fold the right
corner up to cover
the left one.

7

Unfold to
step 3.

8
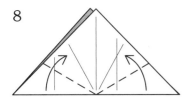

Fold the two bottom corners
up so that their edges lie
along the creases made in
steps 5 and 6.

9
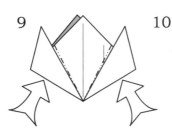

Reverse-fold the edges
into the model.

10
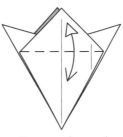

Crease through
one layer only.

11
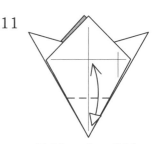

Fold and unfold.

12

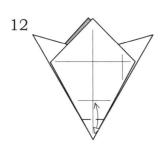

Fold and unfold.

13

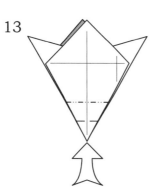

Double-sink the bottom point, using the existing creases as a guide.

14

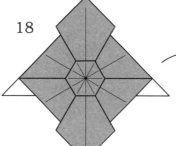

Fold one flap up so that its edge touches the intersection shown.

15

Repeat on the left, and on both the right and left in back.

16

Fold the two remaining flaps over the front flaps.

17

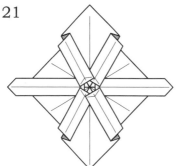

Fold one of the points at the top downward and open the model out flat.

18

It looks like this. Turn the paper over.

19

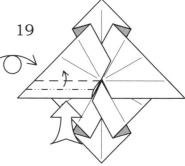

Symmetrically spread-squash the flap shown.

20

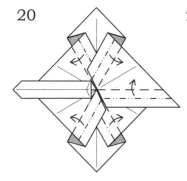

Repeat on the other five similar flaps.

21

Like this. Turn the paper over.

22

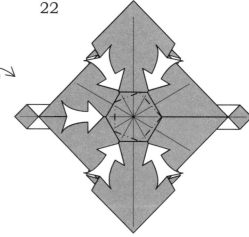

Carefully sink five corners of the central hexagon. Note that each sink is asymmetric, so that the result is a pentagon. Also note that the point of the pentagon goes toward the side, rather than the top.

23

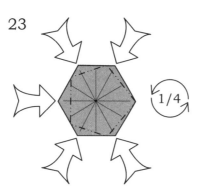

Close-up view of the sinks. Rotate the model 1/4 turn counterclockwise.

24

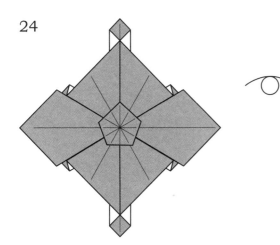

The long axis of the model should be vertical. Turn the paper over from side to side.

25

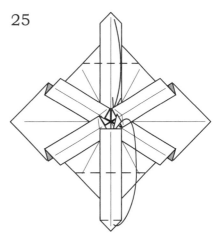

Fold the top and bottom points to the center and tuck their tips into the pockets formed by overlapping spread-squashed flaps.

26

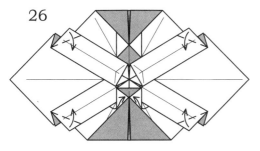

Fold the two upper corners down and the two lower corners up; tuck the sides of the lower central flap under the flaps to either side.

27

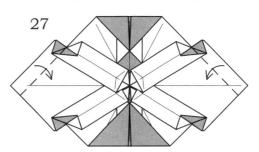

Fold the upper side edges down.

28

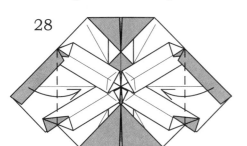

Fold the sides in.

29

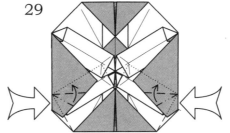

Swivel-fold the sides upward so that the mountain fold is aligned with the edge indicated by the x-ray line.

30

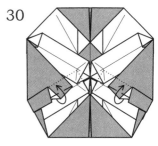

Tuck the colored flaps underneath the edges indicated by the x-ray line.

31

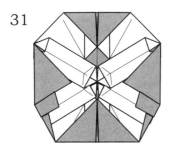

Like this. Turn the paper over from side to side.

32

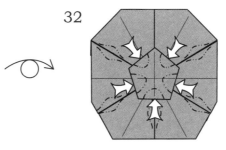

Shape the sides of the central pentagon with mountain folds. Mountain-fold the edges radiating out from the center to create the appearance of holes.

33

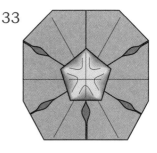

Sand Dollar

Atlantic Purple Sea Urchin

The Atlantic Purple Sea Urchin (*Arbacia punctulata*) lives on rocky coasts and shell bottoms from the low-tide line to waters 200 meters deep, and is responsible for much erosion of softer rocks and the production of sand. It has five very strong teeth in its mouth, which is located on the underside of the body. These teeth are used to rasp algae off rock surfaces and, if the rock is soft, some of it comes away as well. There are many species worldwide that range in color from delicate pink to powder blue; all are edible and are considered delicacies in Japan and France.

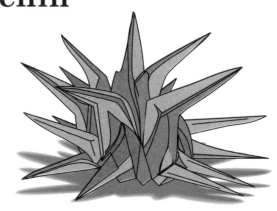

1

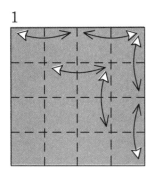

Crease the paper into fourths vertically and horizontally.

2

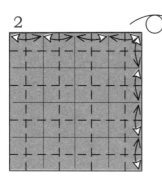

Crease it into eighths vertically and horizontally. Turn the paper over.

3

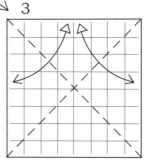

Crease the diagonals.

4

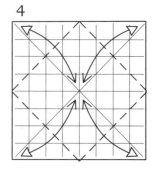

Bring the corners to the center, crease, and unfold.

5

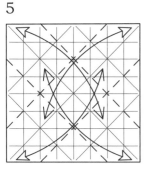

Add more diagonal creases.

6

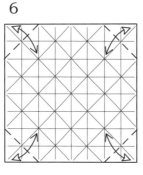

And more.

7

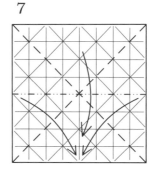

Precreasing complete. Fold a Waterbomb Base.

8

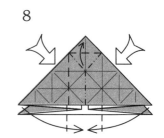

Push in the sides of the top pair of flaps; swing the new flap created over to the right.

9

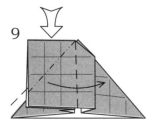

Squash-fold the flap.

10

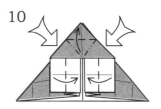

Petal-fold the edge.

11

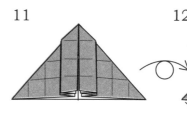

Like this. Turn the paper over.

12

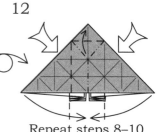

Repeat steps 8–10 on this side.

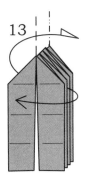
13

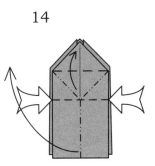
14

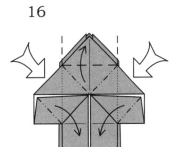
15

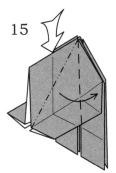
16

17

Fold two layers to the left in front and two to the right in back.

Push in the sides of the near layer of paper, so that the edge stands out away from the rest of the model.

Squash-fold the edge.

Petal-fold the edge in the middle of the model and swing the side corners down.

Like this. Turn the paper over.

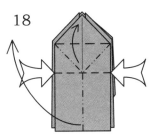
18

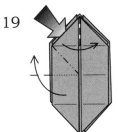
19

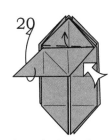
20

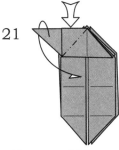
21

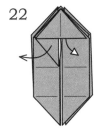
22

Repeat steps 14–16 on this side.

Fold one layer over to the right and swing the bottom left flap upward.

Closed-sink the corner upward.

Reverse-fold the edge shown downward.

Rotate the flap clockwise and pull the loose paper out of the pocket.

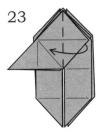
23

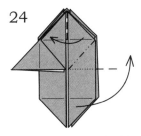
24

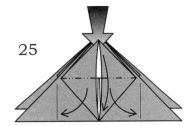
25

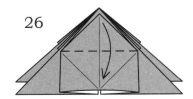
26

Fold one corner to the left.

Repeat steps 19–23 on the right and on the other side.

Squash-fold the point downward.

Fold down one more point.

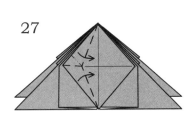
27

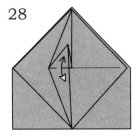
28

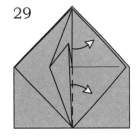
29

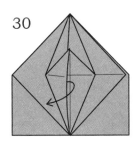
30

Fold a rabbit ear.

Fold the tip of the rabbit ear back and forth several times.

Pull a single layer of paper out from inside the rabbit ear. This is difficult because there are no loose edges to grab, but if you can get it started at the bottom corner, you can work your way up.

Open out the pocket slightly.

Atlantic Purple Sea Urchin 85

31

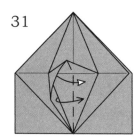

Pull the folded edge out from inside the pocket, turning a layer inside-out as you go.

32

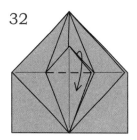

Fold the point down.

33

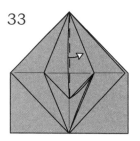

Repeat steps 30–31 on the top.

34

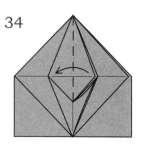

Fold one layer back to the left.

35

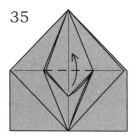

Fold the point upward.

36

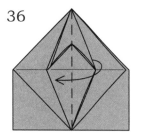

Fold all of the layers to the left.

37

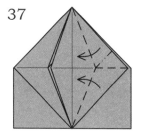

Repeat steps 27–36 on the right.

38

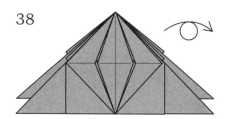

Like this. Turn the model over.

39

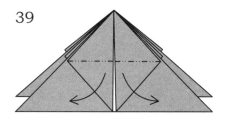

Repeat steps 25–37 on this side.

40

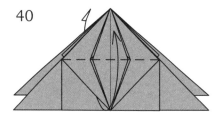

Fold one point up in front and one up in back.

41

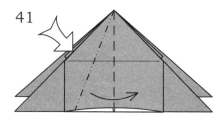

Squash-fold the indicated edge, but flatten only its upper half.

42

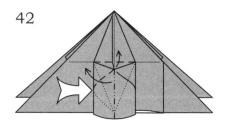

Pinch the sides of the lower part of the squash and swing the resulting flap to the left.

43

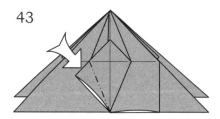

Reverse-fold the edge.

44

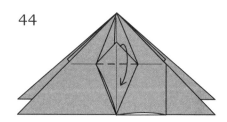

Fold the point down.

45

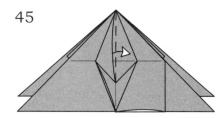

Pull the folded edge out of the pocket as in steps 30–31.

46

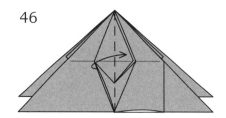

Fold all layers to the right.

47

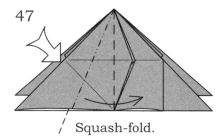

Squash-fold.

48

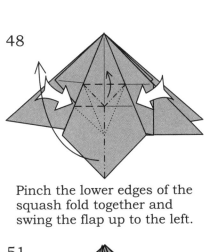

Pinch the lower edges of the squash fold together and swing the flap up to the left.

49

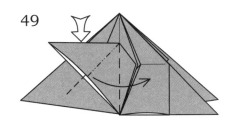

Squash-fold the new flap.

50

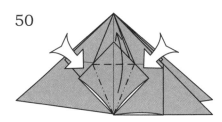

Petal-fold.

51

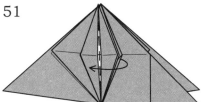

Fold all layers to the left.

52

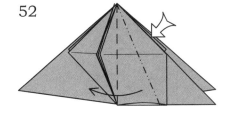

Repeat steps 41–51 on the right.

53

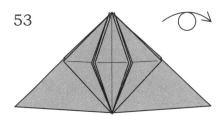

Turn the paper over.

54

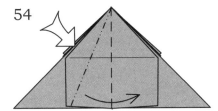

Repeat steps 41–52.

55

Rotate layers in front and back.

56

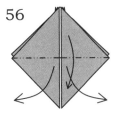

Squash-fold the point downward.

57

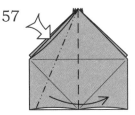

Repeat steps 41–45.

58

Fold the layers back to the left.

59

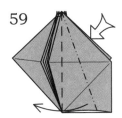

Repeat 41–46 on the right.

60

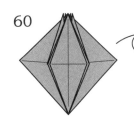

Turn the model over.

61

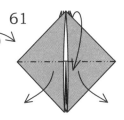

Repeat steps 55–60.

62

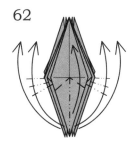

Reverse-fold all 12 points at the bottom upward. Fan the layers in all directions so that the model becomes conical.

63

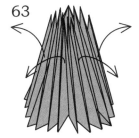

Rabbit-ear each of the 25 points outward and adjust them to point in all directions.

64

Detail of a single point. Fold a rabbit ear.

65

Like this.

66

Atlantic Purple Sea Urchin

Horseshoe Crab

The Horseshoe Crab (*Limulus polyphemus*) is the only American example of its subclass, the *Xiphosura*. The larvae are called "trilobite larvae" because of their resemblance to trilobite fossils, and it is believed that the trilobites were the ancestors of the *Xiphosura*. Horseshoe crabs have relatively simple eyes, which has resulted in their being extensively used in neurophysiological research.

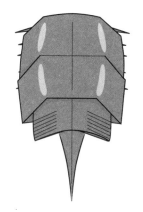
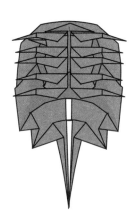

1
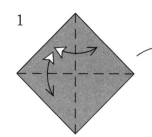

Crease the vertical and horizontal diagonals. Turn the paper over.

2
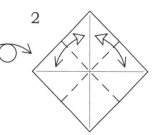

Fold the paper in half and unfold.

3
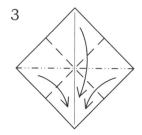

Fold a Preliminary Fold.

4
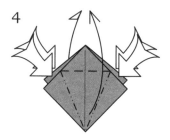

Petal-fold to make a Bird Base.

5
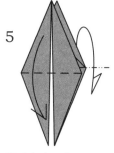

Fold the front and back flaps down.

6
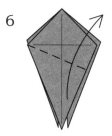

Fold the front flap up and to the right at right angles to the right edge.

7
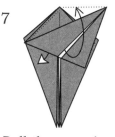

Pull the raw edge upward and release the loose paper under the flap.

8
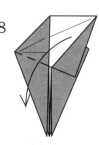

Fold the flap back down.

9
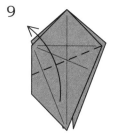

Fold the flap up to the left.

10
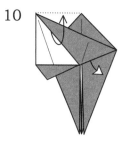

Pull out the trapped layer.

11
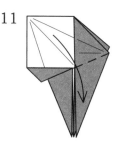

And fold the flap back down.

12
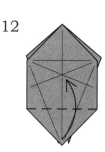

Fold the bottom point up to the intersection of the two creases.

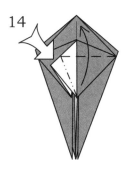

13

Bring the lower corners together, folding on existing creases.

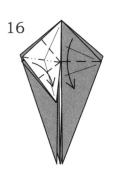

14

Squash-fold.

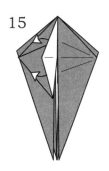

15

Pull out the trapped layer of paper.

16

Fold half of a Preliminary Fold with the single layer.

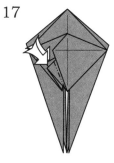

17

Reverse-fold both edges.

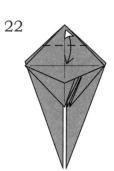

18

Turn the model over.

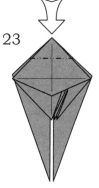

19

Repeat steps 6–17 on this side.

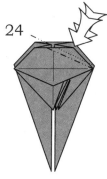

20

Fold the bundle of layers over to the right.

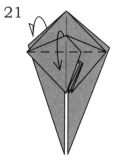

21

Fold the layer down in front and behind.

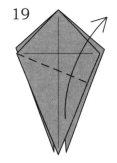

22

Fold and unfold.

23

Sink the point downward.

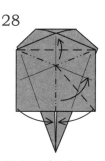

24

Sink two corners. They must be done simultaneously.

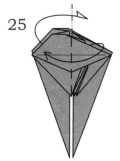

25

Fold one layer to the left in front and one to the right in back.

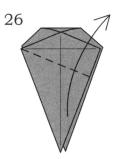

26

Repeat steps 6–11 on this flap.

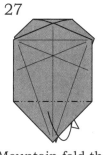

27

Mountain-fold the point underneath.

28

Bring the lower corners together as in step 13.

29

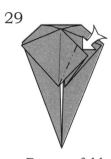

Reverse-fold
the edge.

30

Valley-fold the
two lower
corners up to
the sides.

31

Reverse-fold
the corners.

32

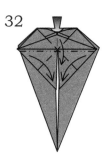

Fold a Preliminary
Fold through all of
the thick layers.

33

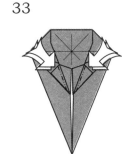

Reverse-fold
four edges.

34

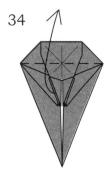

Lift the top pair of points
upward as far as
possible, letting the other
four pairs fan out.

35

Like this.

36

Press in between the
points and flatten them
all downward, spacing
them evenly. The dotted
line indicates where the
top pair folds down.

37

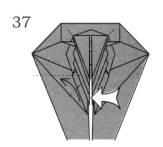

Like this. Reverse-
fold the lowest
corner out to the
side.

38

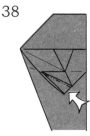

Only the lowest point
is shown in steps
38–40. Reverse-fold
the lower edge.

39

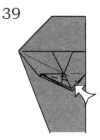

Reverse-fold a
single edge.

40

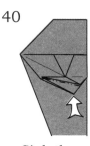

Sink the
corner and
edges.

41

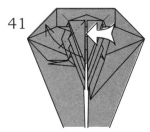

Reverse-fold the remaining
four points on this side out
to the side (only the top one
is shown here).

42

Reverse-fold both edges
of each point to narrow
it. Repeat on the other
four points.

43

Tuck the upper
half of each leg
inside the lower
half.

44

Crimp each
leg downward.

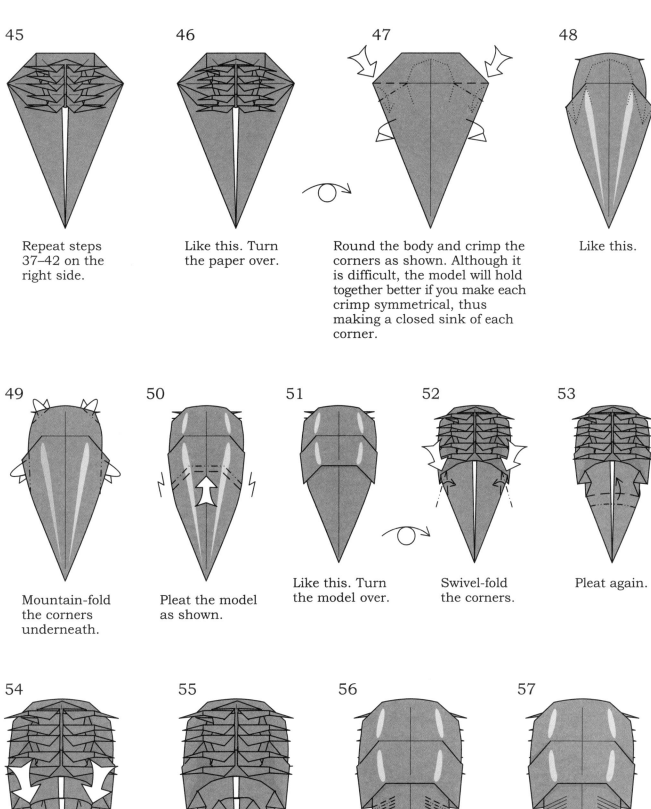

45

Repeat steps 37–42 on the right side.

46

Like this. Turn the paper over.

47

Round the body and crimp the corners as shown. Although it is difficult, the model will hold together better if you make each crimp symmetrical, thus making a closed sink of each corner.

48

Like this.

49

Mountain-fold the corners underneath.

50

Pleat the model as shown.

51

Like this. Turn the model over.

52

Swivel-fold the corners.

53

Pleat again.

54

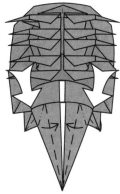

Swivel-fold the corners again.

55

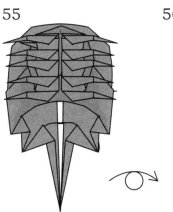

Like this. Turn the model over.

56

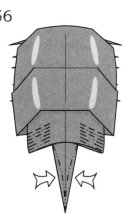

Pinch the tail to shape it and pleat the sides of the shell.

57

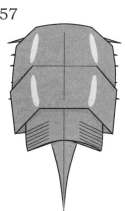

Horseshoe Crab

Hermit Crab

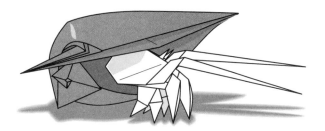

Hermit Crabs are represented by two families, *Coenbitoidea* and *Panguroidea*. Representatives of both families are notable in that they live inside the deserted shell of another animal, typically a whelk or snail. The rear of the hermit crab is soft and its hind legs are atrophied, except for a single pair used to hold the crab inside the shell. The crab keeps the shell until it outgrows it and must find another. Hermit crabs come in a rainbow of colors and make very good pets as they are clean and require little attention.

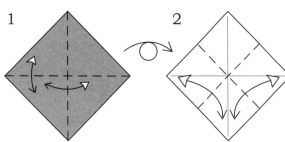

1

Crease the diagonals. Turn the model over.

2

Crease in half and unfold.

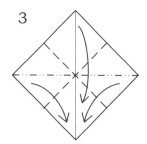

3

Fold a Preliminary Fold.

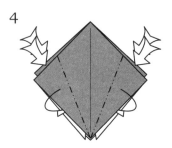

4

Enlarged view. Reverse-fold four corners to make a Bird Base.

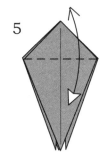

5

Enlarged view. Fold and unfold.

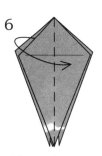

6

Fold one layer over from left to right.

7

Crease.

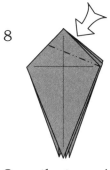

8

Open the top point out and sink it on the existing creases.

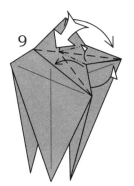

9

In progress.

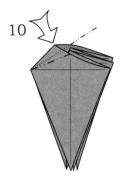

10

Sink the remaining corner.

11

Fold one layer over to the left.

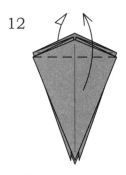

12

Fold one point up in front and in back.

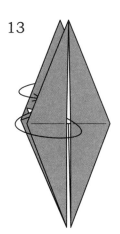

13

Color-change
both of the
flaps on the left.

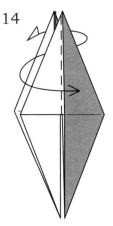

14

Fold one layer from
left to right in front
and one from right
to left in back.

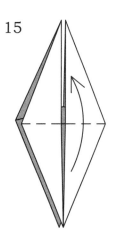

15

Lift up one
point.

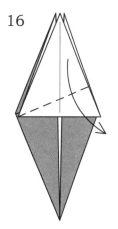

16

Fold the point
down along a line
perpendicular to
the right edge.

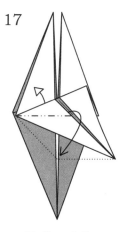

17

Pull out the
loose paper.

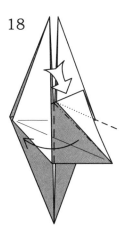

18

Squash-fold.

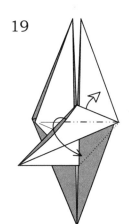

19

Pull out the
loose paper.

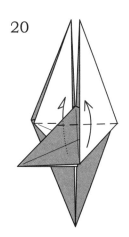

20

Outside-reverse-fold
the flap upward.

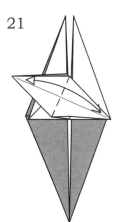

21

Fold and unfold.

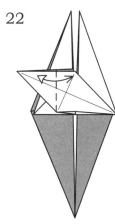

22

Fold and unfold.

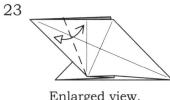

23

Enlarged view.
Fold and unfold.

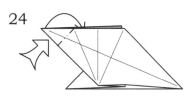

24

Reverse-fold
the corner.

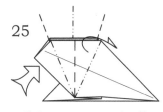

25

Crimp symmetrically.

26

Reverse-fold three
hidden corners.

27

Reverse-fold the
three corners again.

28

Fold one white layer over to the left in front and one colored layer over to the right behind.

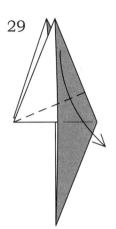

29

Fold one point down along a line perpendicular to the right edge.

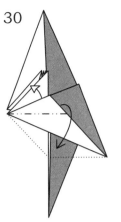

30

Pull out the loose paper.

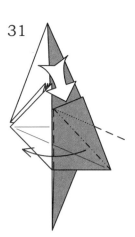

31

Squash-fold.

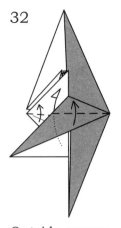

32

Outside-reverse-fold the flap.

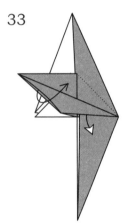

33

Pull out the loose paper.

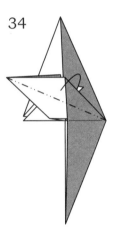

34

Mountain-fold one layer inside.

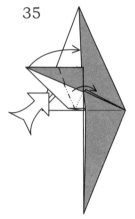

35

Squash-fold the flap (note the interior layers that must also be squash-folded).

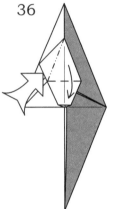

36

Petal-fold the left half of the flap.

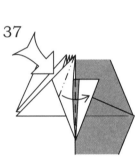

37

Enlarged view. Squash-sink the corner.

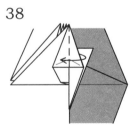

38

Fold one layer back to the left.

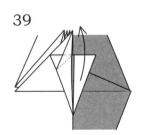

39

Stretch the point upward as far as it will go.

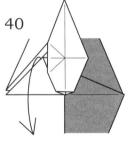

40

Fold down one layer from the left; the long flap comes too.

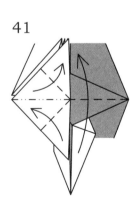

41

Form half of a Preliminary Fold from the left side and fold the point upward.

42

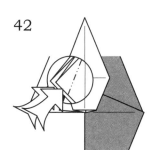

Reverse-fold the two corners.

43

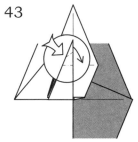

Crimp the tiny hidden point with two reverse folds.

44

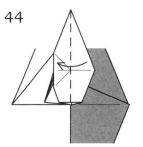

Fold one layer from right to left.

45

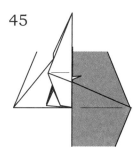

Repeat steps 29–45 on the other side.

46

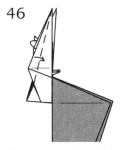

Narrow each of the two long points with valley folds.

47

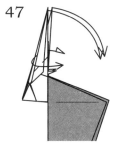

Outside-reverse-fold.

48

Sink the edges to narrow the points.

49

Inside-reverse-fold.

50

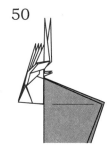

Like this.

51

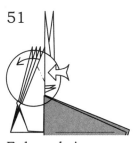

Enlarged view. Reverse-fold the next point. Repeat behind.

52

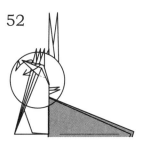

Outside-reverse-fold the point. Repeat behind.

53

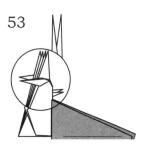

Like this.

54

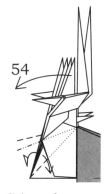

Crimp the group of four points downward.

55

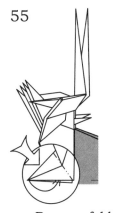

Reverse-fold the middle corner.

56

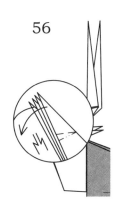

Crimp the outer pair of points downward.

57

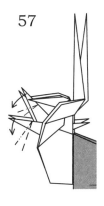

Crimp the tips of all four points downward.

58

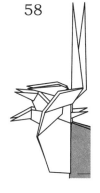

Like this.

59

Fold one layer from the right to the left, and rotate the body of the crab away from you.

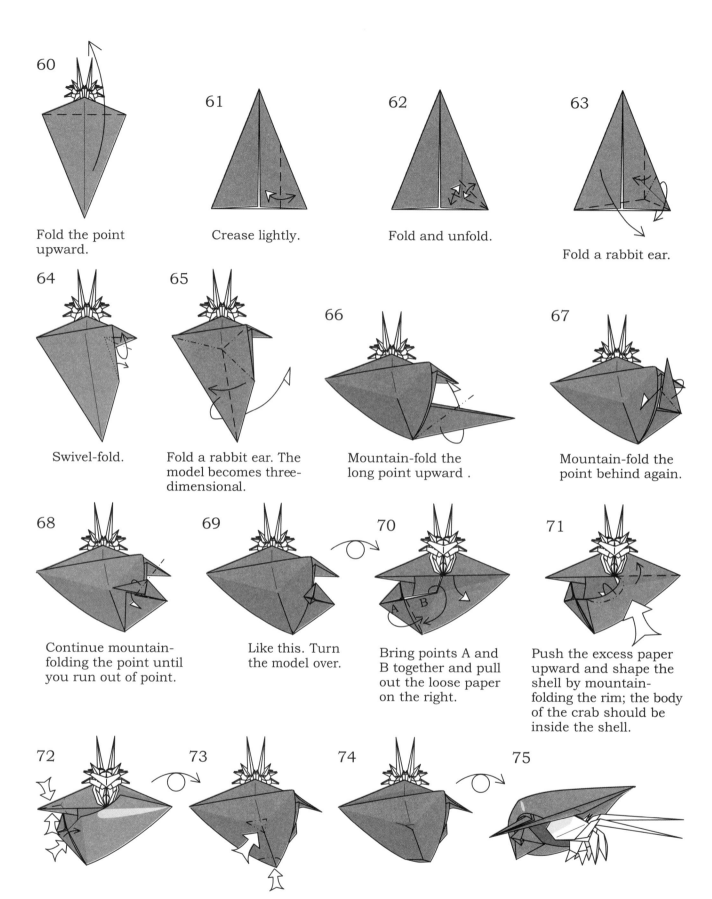

60 Fold the point upward.

61 Crease lightly.

62 Fold and unfold.

63 Fold a rabbit ear.

64 Swivel-fold.

65 Fold a rabbit ear. The model becomes three-dimensional.

66 Mountain-fold the long point upward .

67 Mountain-fold the point behind again.

68 Continue mountain-folding the point until you run out of point.

69 Like this. Turn the model over.

70 Bring points A and B together and pull out the loose paper on the right.

71 Push the excess paper upward and shape the shell by mountain-folding the rim; the body of the crab should be inside the shell.

72 Pinch the spine on the left side of the shell and shape the left side.

73 Sink the two corners shown; this helps the shell to keep its shape.

74 Like this. Turn the model over.

75 Hermit Crab

Fiddler Crab

Fiddler crabs are members of the genus *Uca* and are named for the single enlarged pincer possessed by the male of the species. They use their large claw primarily for courtship displays and battles with other males. If the claw breaks off, as occasionally happens, it will regenerate as a small claw while the other claw enlarges to take its place. Most fiddler crabs are found in the mangrove swamps of the tropics, where they eat the detritus left by the receding tide. They are among the most numerous inhabitants of the mangroves and as a result, are the prey of almost every larger creature.

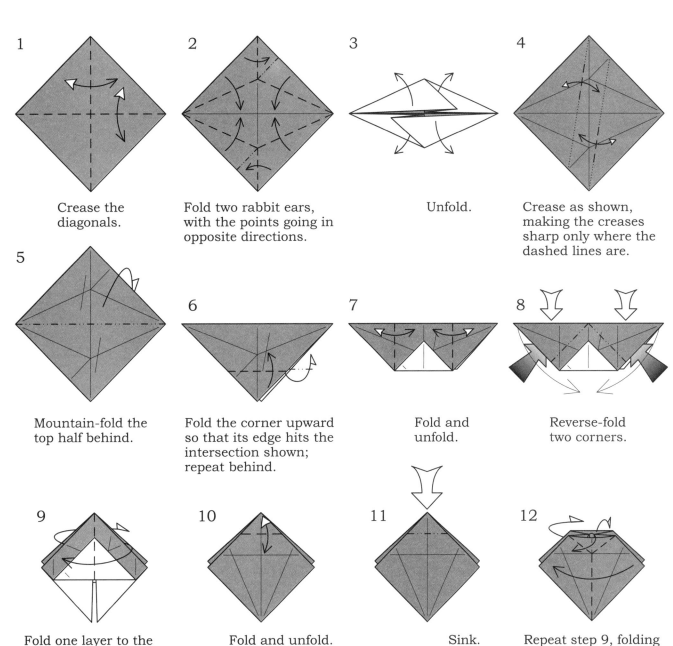

1

Crease the diagonals.

2

Fold two rabbit ears, with the points going in opposite directions.

3

Unfold.

4

Crease as shown, making the creases sharp only where the dashed lines are.

5

Mountain-fold the top half behind.

6

Fold the corner upward so that its edge hits the intersection shown; repeat behind.

7

Fold and unfold.

8

Reverse-fold two corners.

9

Fold one layer to the left in front and one to the right in back.

10

Fold and unfold.

11

Sink.

12

Repeat step 9, folding down the top edge in front and back.

13

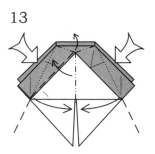

Squash-fold the sides and swing the white flap over to the left.

14

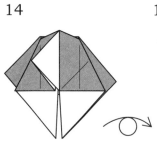

Like this. Turn the paper over.

15

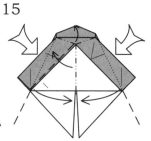

Repeat step 10 on this side.

16

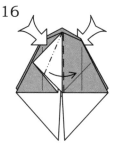

Squash-fold. Repeat behind.

17

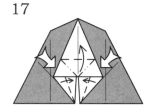

Enlarged view. Petal-fold.

18

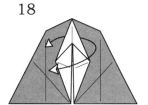

Unwrap one layer.

19

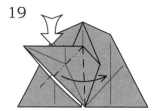

Squash-fold.

20

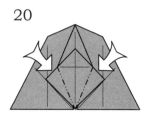

Reverse-fold the edges.

21

Enlarged view. Fold and unfold.

22

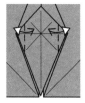

Fold and unfold.

23

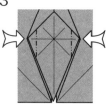

Sink the corners on the creases you just made.

24

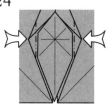

Sink the next pair of corners to the same depth.

25

Sink the top corner.

26

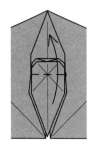

Fold the point up.

27

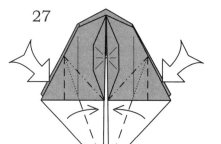

Reverse-fold the edges.

28

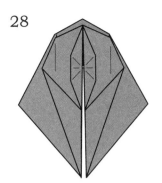

Repeat steps 17–27 behind.

29

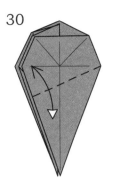

Fold one layer over.

30

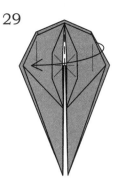

Fold and unfold.

31

Fold upward.

32

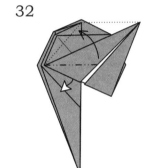

Pull out the loose paper.

33

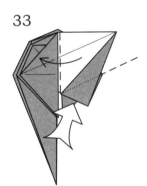

Squash-fold.

34

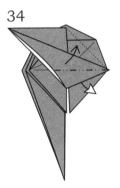

Pull out some loose paper.

35

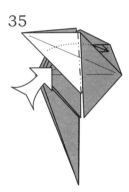

Reverse-fold the point over to the right.

36

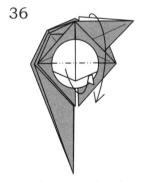

Fold the top point down; at the same time swing the hidden point up inside the model.

37

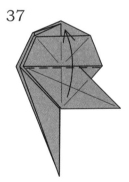

Fold the point back up.

38

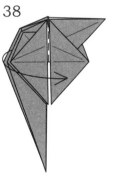

Fold one layer over to the right.

39

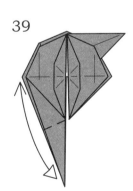

Fold and unfold.

40

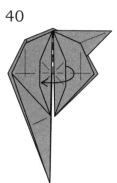

Fold one layer
over to the left.

41

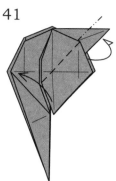

Fold one layer
up to the left;
repeat behind.

42

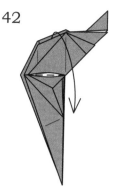

Fold the top down
and flatten it.

43

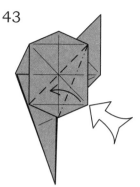

Spread-sink the
indicated point.

44

Close the sink up,
incorporating the
reverse fold at the
bottom.

45

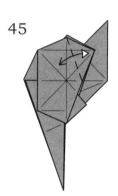

Fold and unfold.

46

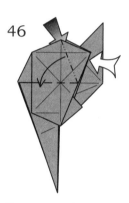

Open out the upper
edges of the point to
form a three-sided
pyramid.

47

Push in the right side of
the pyramid while
reverse-folding its upper
edge to the right.

48

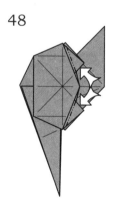

Reverse-fold
both edges.

49

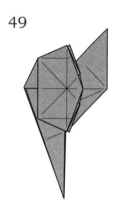

Like this. Turn
the paper over.

50

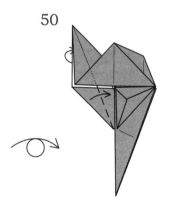

Valley-fold
one layer.

51

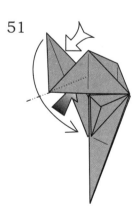

Reverse-fold the
top corner down.

55

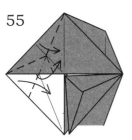

Fold a different
kind of rabbit ear.

56

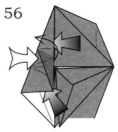

Pull the upper edge
to the left and sink
the lower edge.

57

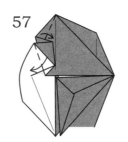

Tuck the two-toned
corner into the
pocket and flatten.

58

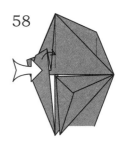

In progress.

59

Tuck the corner
into the pocket.

60

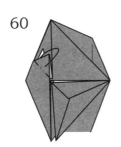

Tuck the corner
into the pocket.

61

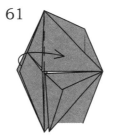

Fold one corner
to the right.

62

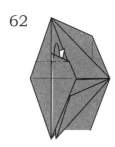

Mountain-fold
the corner.

63

Fold the layer
back to the left.

64

Swivel the
right point
upward.

65

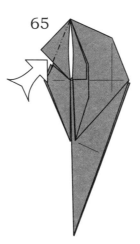

Reverse-fold
the edge.

66

Fold all of the
narrow layers
over to the left.

67

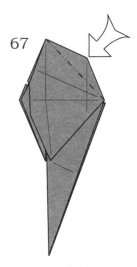

Sink the
corner.

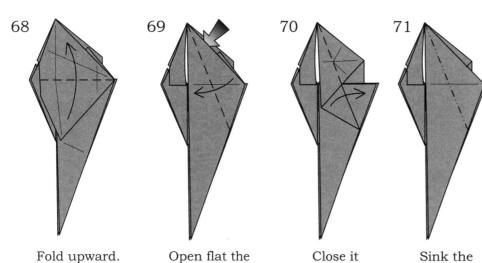

68 Fold upward.

69 Open flat the sunk corner.

70 Close it back up.

71 Sink the corner.

72 Squash-fold the corner asymmetrically, with three layers going to the right and one to the left.

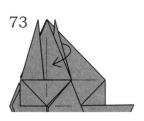

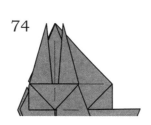

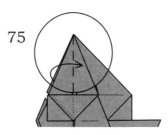

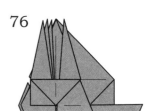

73 Lift the right point up to release it.

74 Like this.

75 Behind the two points, fold one layer over to the right, releasing two more points.

76 Like this.

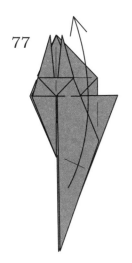

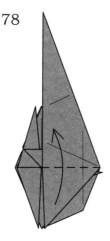

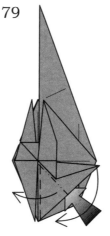

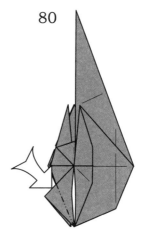

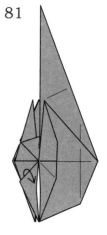

77 Fold the long point upward.

78 Fold one layer upward.

79 Swivel the right point downward.

80 Reverse-fold the edge.

81 Bring the hidden point to the front.

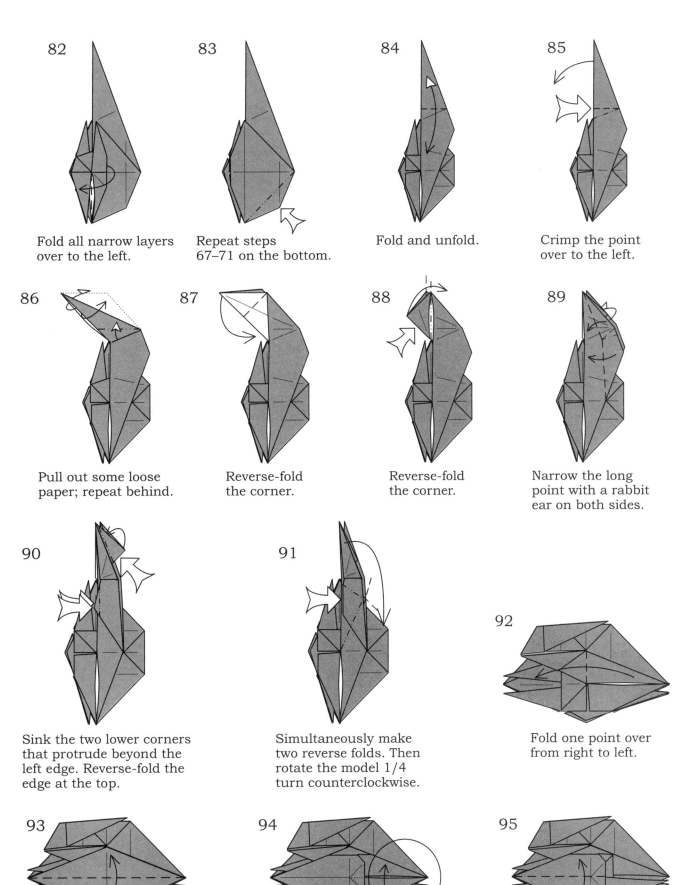

82

Fold all narrow layers
over to the left.

83

Repeat steps
67–71 on the bottom.

84

Fold and unfold.

85

Crimp the point
over to the left.

86

Pull out some loose
paper; repeat behind.

87

Reverse-fold
the corner.

88

Reverse-fold
the corner.

89

Narrow the long
point with a rabbit
ear on both sides.

90

Sink the two lower corners
that protrude beyond the
left edge. Reverse-fold the
edge at the top.

91

Simultaneously make
two reverse folds. Then
rotate the model 1/4
turn counterclockwise.

92

Fold one point over
from right to left.

93

Fold one layer up.

94

Fold one layer up
behind the point.

95

Fold one layer up.

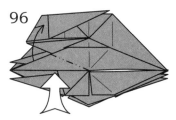

96

Reverse-fold the point upward to match the larger one.

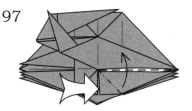

97

Squash-fold the corner symmetrically.

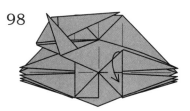

98

Fold one layer downward.

99

Tuck the layer underneath the raw edge.

100

Swing two points over to the right.

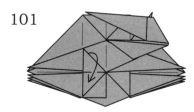

101

Repeat steps 98–99 on this flap.

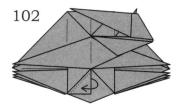

102

Tuck the corner into the pocket behind it.

103

Fold the large point over to the left.

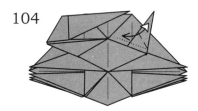

104

Fold the right edge of the point down to the dotted line and unfold.

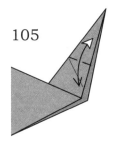

105

Fold and unfold.

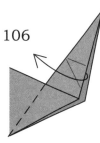

106

Open the flap.

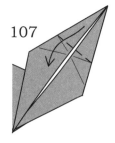

107

Fold the tip down.

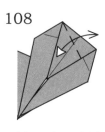

108

Fold and unfold.

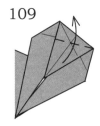

109

Fold the point upward so that its left edge is aligned with the layer behind it.

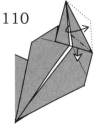

110

Pull out the loose paper.

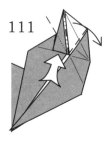

111

Squash-fold.

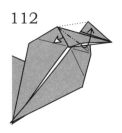

112

Pull out the loose paper.

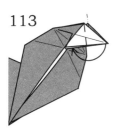

113

Reverse-fold.

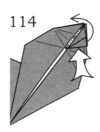

114

Reverse-fold.

115

Close the flap up.

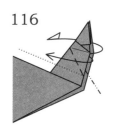

116

Outside-reverse-fold on the creases you made in step 104.

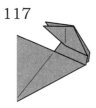

117

Like this.

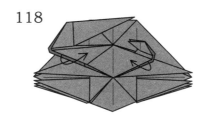

118

Tuck the "elbows" of the claws into the pockets beneath them (similar to steps 98–99).

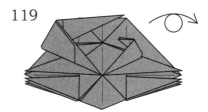

119

Like this. Turn the model over.

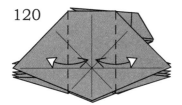

120

Fold and unfold.

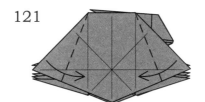

121

Fold the upper edges in to the creases you just made.

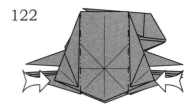

122

Carefully closed-sink the corners into the body.

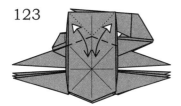

123

Fold and unfold.

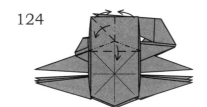

124

Crimp the body and swing the two points toward each other.

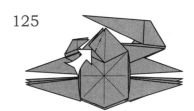

125

Reverse-fold the edge.

126

Spread the two
points at the top
out to the sides.

127

Reverse-fold
the edges.

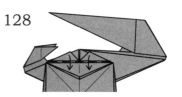

128

Fold the two thick
edges downward.

129

Reverse-fold the left side and
mountain-fold the right side
at the top of the body.

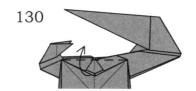

130

Fold all the
layers upward.

131

Twist the two trapped
points forward so that
they point up and out.

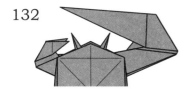

132

Like this.

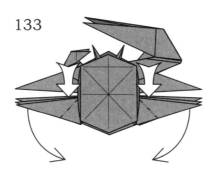

133

Reverse-fold the thick pair
of points downward.

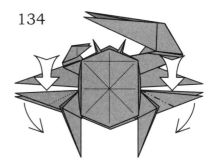

134

Reverse-fold the next pair of
points downward (note that
the left one is inside another
point).

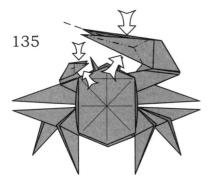

135

Pinch both pincers of each
claw to shape them.

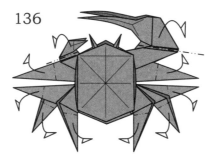

136

Mountain-fold all of the legs
and claws downward and puff
up the body to shape it.

137

Fiddler Crab

California Rock Lobster

The California Rock Lobster (*Panulirus interruptus*) does not have large pincers like its more familiar cousin, the Northern, or Maine Lobster. Instead, it has long, spiny antennae with which it stuns its prey with powerful blows. It is fished commercially in California and Baja California.

For best results on your first effort, use a 12" square of foil-backed paper. This may also be wet-folded to good effect; use a thin paper and be careful not to tear the back.

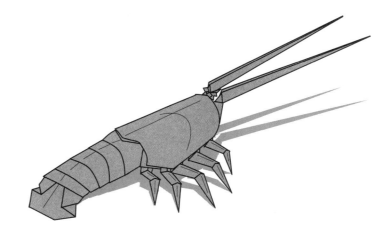

1

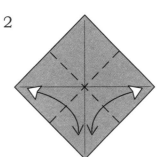

2

3

Fold a Preliminary Fold.

4

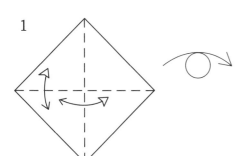

Squash-fold.

5

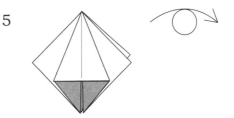

Like this. Turn the paper over.

6

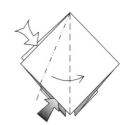

Squash-fold again.

7

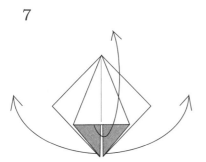

Unfold completely.

8

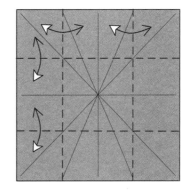

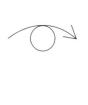

Crease and turn the paper over.

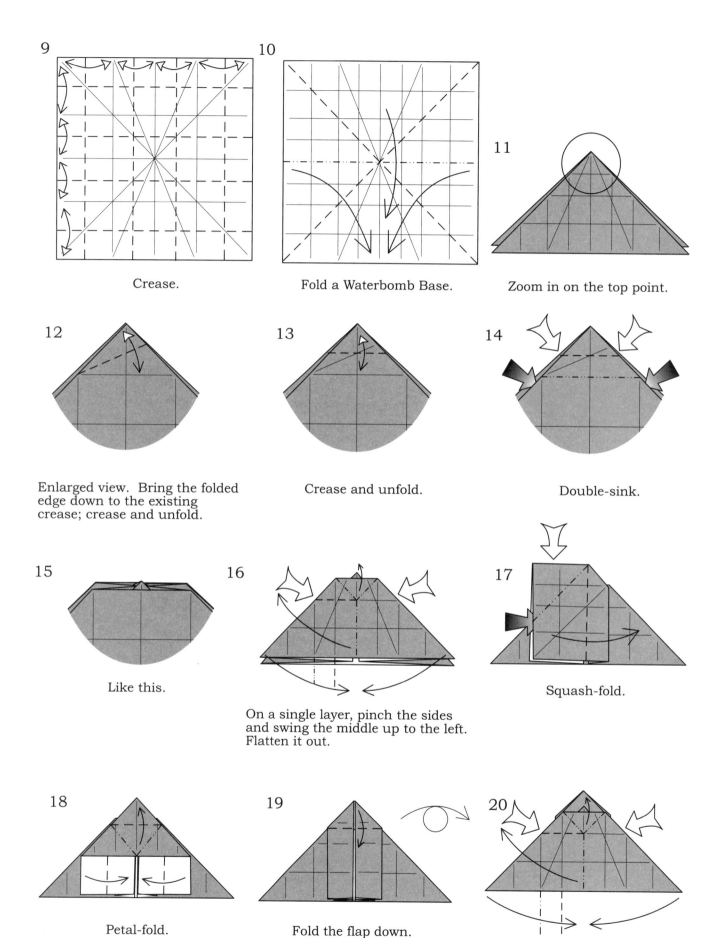

9

Crease.

10

Fold a Waterbomb Base.

11

Zoom in on the top point.

12

Enlarged view. Bring the folded edge down to the existing crease; crease and unfold.

13

Crease and unfold.

14

Double-sink.

15

Like this.

16

On a single layer, pinch the sides and swing the middle up to the left. Flatten it out.

17

Squash-fold.

18

Petal-fold.

19

Fold the flap down.

20

Repeat steps 16-19 on this side.

21

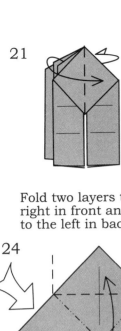

Fold two layers to the right in front and two to the left in back.

22

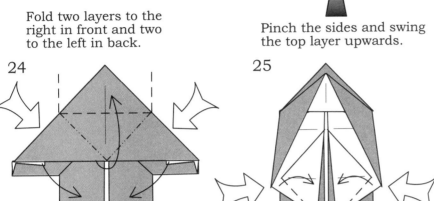

Pinch the sides and swing the top layer upwards.

23

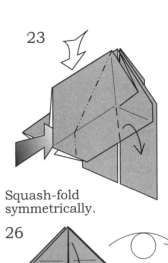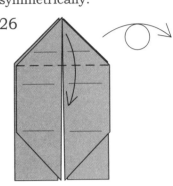

Squash-fold symmetrically.

24

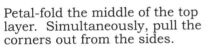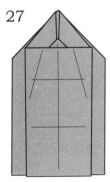

Petal-fold the middle of the top layer. Simultaneously, pull the corners out from the sides.

25

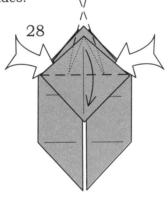

Flatten the paper out.

26

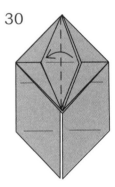

Fold one layer down. Turn the paper over.

27

Repeat steps 22-26 on this side.

28

Fold one layer down and petal-fold the interior layers.

29

Pull a double layer out from the inside of the pocket (this is hard).

30

Fold the layer back to the left.

31

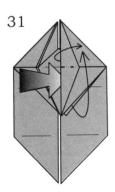

Bring the point back up and undo the remaining half of the petal fold.

32

Turn the paper over.

33

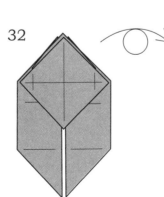

Repeat steps 28-31 on this side.

34

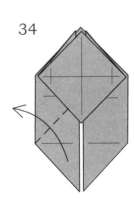

Valley-fold.

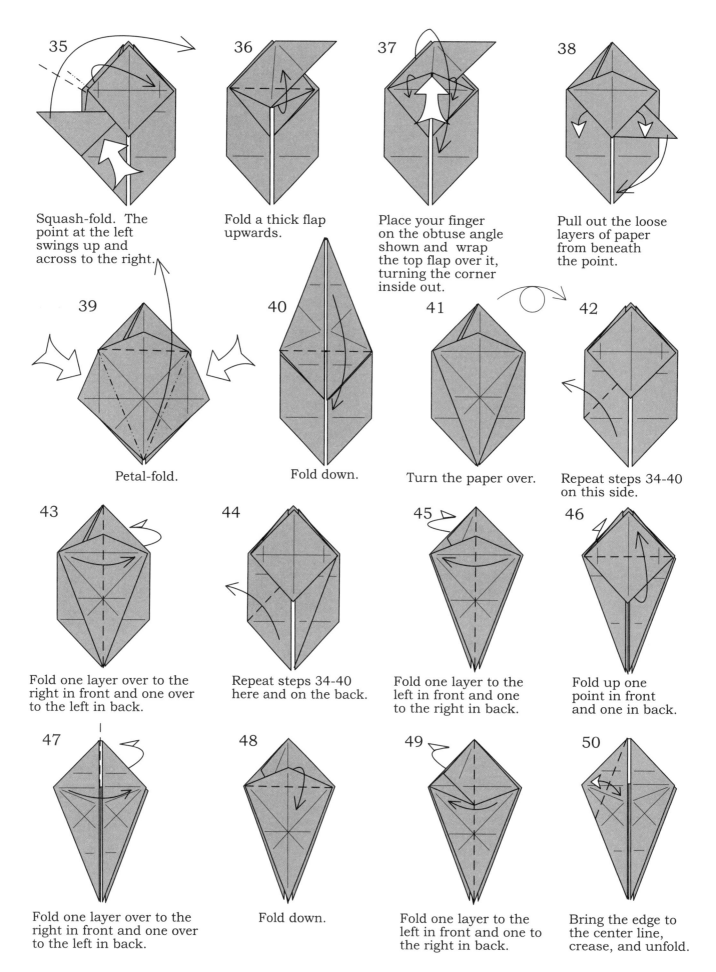

35 Squash-fold. The point at the left swings up and across to the right.

36 Fold a thick flap upwards.

37 Place your finger on the obtuse angle shown and wrap the top flap over it, turning the corner inside out.

38 Pull out the loose layers of paper from beneath the point.

39 Petal-fold.

40 Fold down.

41 Turn the paper over.

42 Repeat steps 34-40 on this side.

43 Fold one layer over to the right in front and one over to the left in back.

44 Repeat steps 34-40 here and on the back.

45 Fold one layer to the left in front and one to the right in back.

46 Fold up one point in front and one in back.

47 Fold one layer over to the right in front and one over to the left in back.

48 Fold down.

49 Fold one layer to the left in front and one to the right in back.

50 Bring the edge to the center line, crease, and unfold.

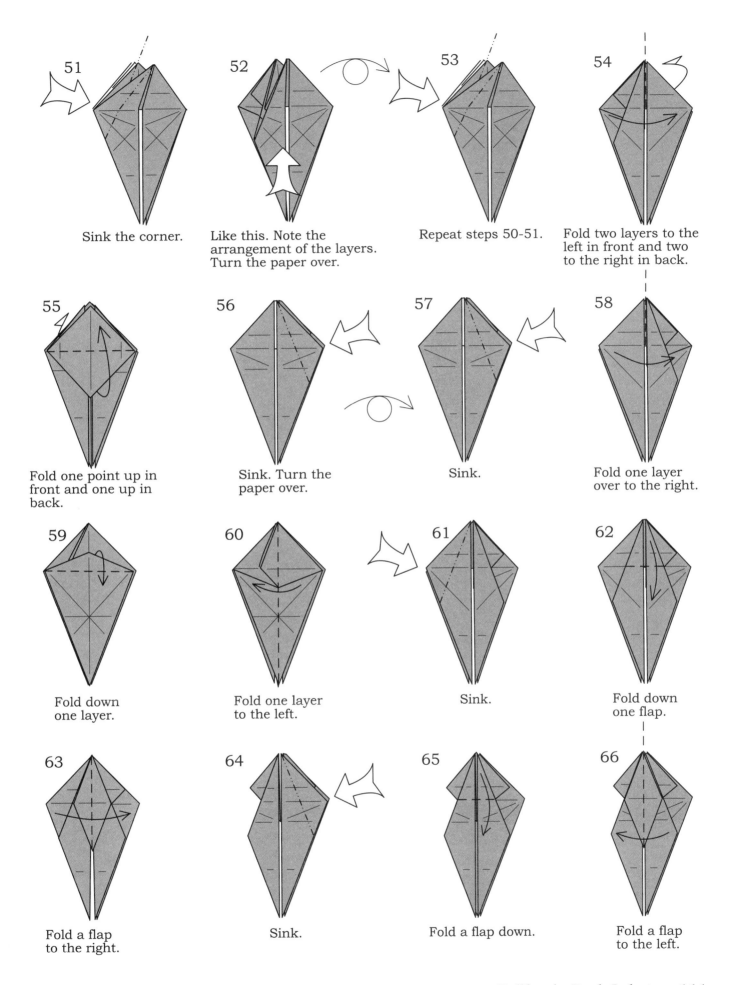

51 Sink the corner.

52 Like this. Note the arrangement of the layers. Turn the paper over.

53 Repeat steps 50-51.

54 Fold two layers to the left in front and two to the right in back.

55 Fold one point up in front and one up in back.

56 Sink. Turn the paper over.

57 Sink.

58 Fold one layer over to the right.

59 Fold down one layer.

60 Fold one layer to the left.

61 Sink.

62 Fold down one flap.

63 Fold a flap to the right.

64 Sink.

65 Fold a flap down.

66 Fold a flap to the left.

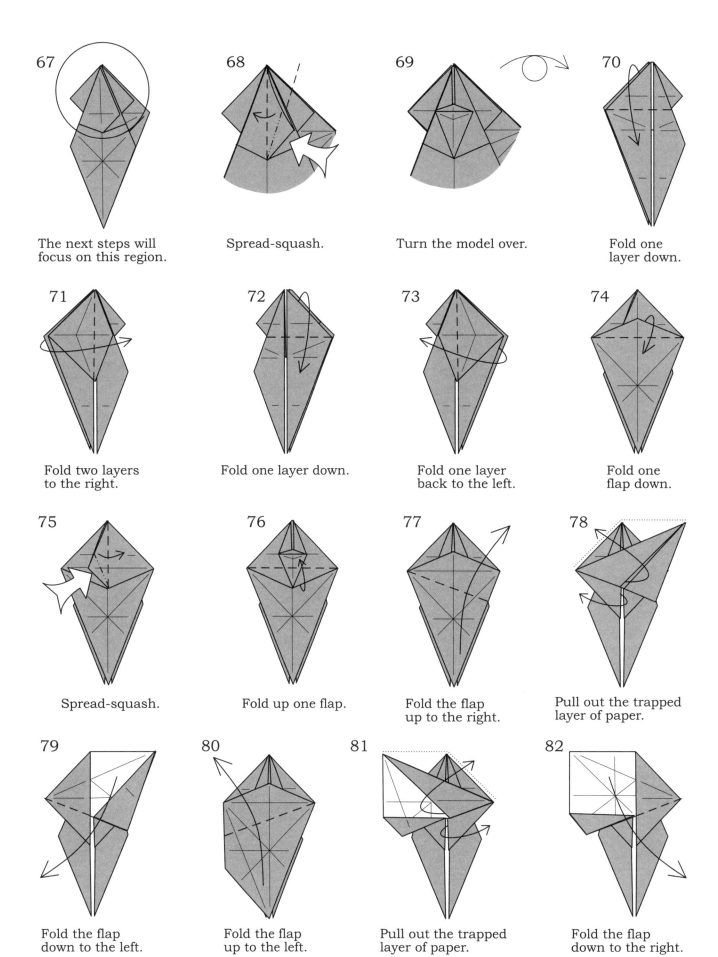

67 The next steps will focus on this region.

68 Spread-squash.

69 Turn the model over.

70 Fold one layer down.

71 Fold two layers to the right.

72 Fold one layer down.

73 Fold one layer back to the left.

74 Fold one flap down.

75 Spread-squash.

76 Fold up one flap.

77 Fold the flap up to the right.

78 Pull out the trapped layer of paper.

79 Fold the flap down to the left.

80 Fold the flap up to the left.

81 Pull out the trapped layer of paper.

82 Fold the flap down to the right.

83

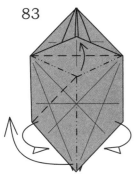

Pinch the sides together
and swing the excess
paper to the left.

84

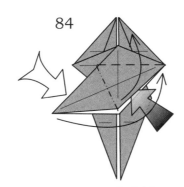

Squash-fold.

85

Fold one layer
over to the left.

86

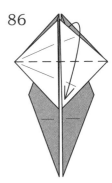

Fold one
layer down.

87

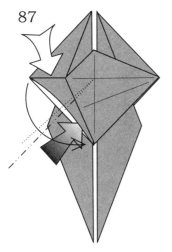

Reverse-fold
the corner.

88

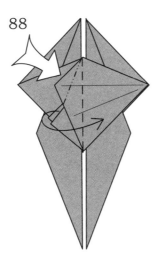

Spread-sink the corner.

89

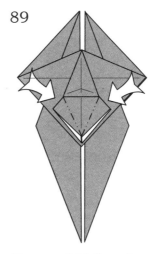

Reverse-fold the edges.

90

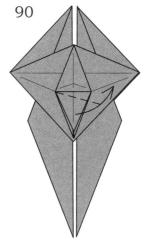

Repeat steps 77–89
on this flap.

91

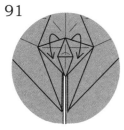

Tuck the blunt
triangle under the
pocket behind.

92

Open out.

93

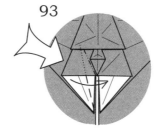

Reverse-fold so that the
edge meets the crease
on the opposite side.

94

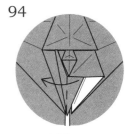

Reverse-fold back on
an existing crease.

95

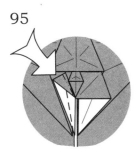

Reverse-fold the edge
in to the center line.

96

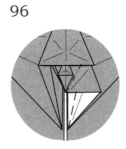

Repeat steps 93–95
on the right.

97

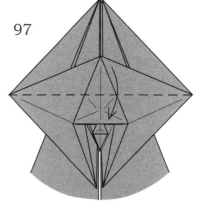

Fold one flap down.

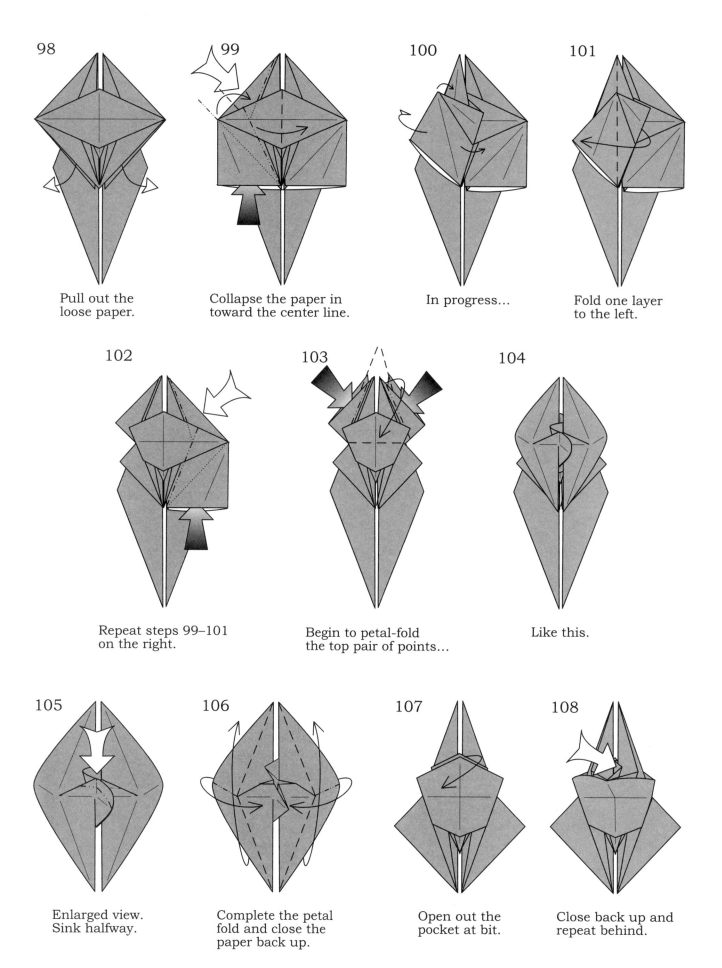

98

Pull out the
loose paper.

99

Collapse the paper in
toward the center line.

100

In progress...

101

Fold one layer
to the left.

102

Repeat steps 99–101
on the right.

103

Begin to petal-fold
the top pair of points...

104

Like this.

105

Enlarged view.
Sink halfway.

106

Complete the petal
fold and close the
paper back up.

107

Open out the
pocket at bit.

108

Close back up and
repeat behind.

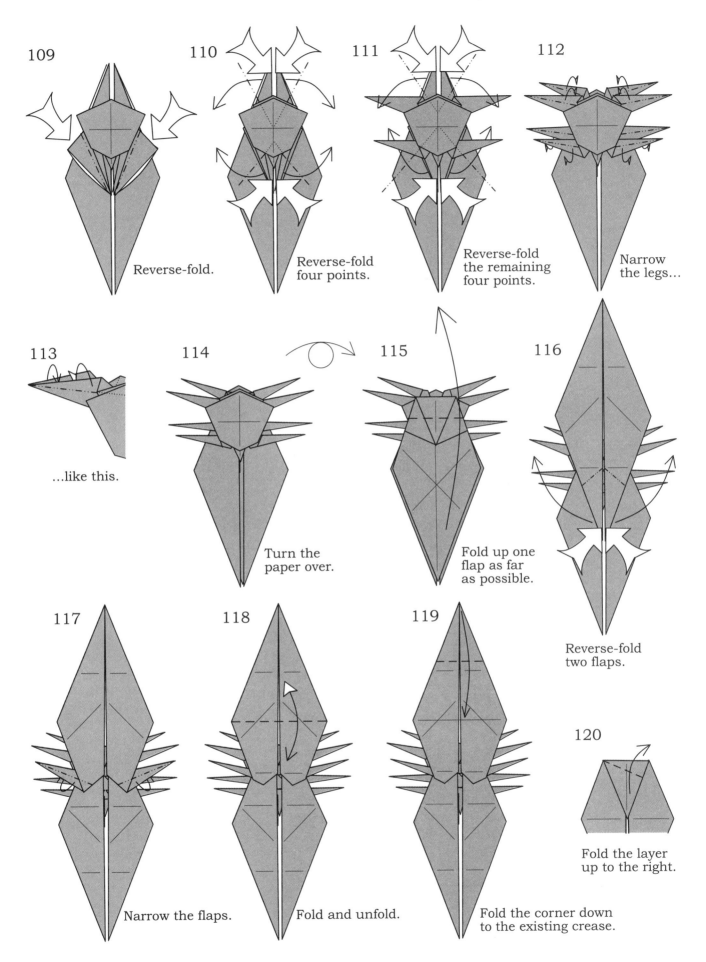

109

Reverse-fold.

110

Reverse-fold
four points.

111

Reverse-fold
the remaining
four points.

112

Narrow
the legs...

113

...like this.

114

Turn the
paper over.

115

Fold up one
flap as far
as possible.

116

Reverse-fold
two flaps.

117

Narrow the flaps.

118

Fold and unfold.

119

Fold the corner down
to the existing crease.

120

Fold the layer
up to the right.

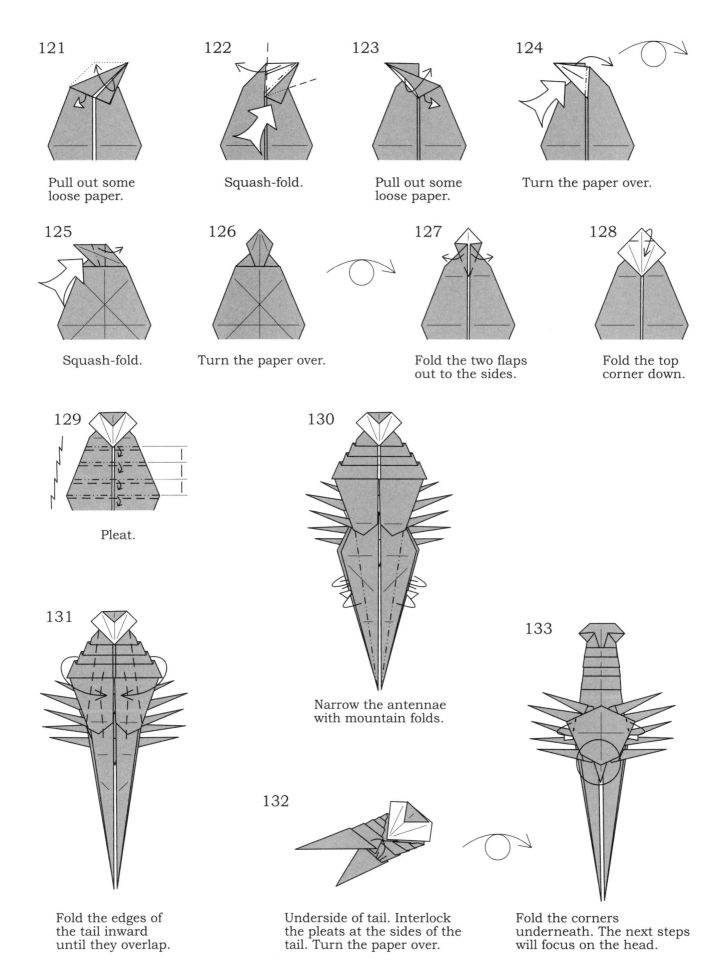

121 Pull out some loose paper.

122 Squash-fold.

123 Pull out some loose paper.

124 Turn the paper over.

125 Squash-fold.

126 Turn the paper over.

127 Fold the two flaps out to the sides.

128 Fold the top corner down.

129 Pleat.

130 Narrow the antennae with mountain folds.

131 Fold the edges of the tail inward until they overlap.

132 Underside of tail. Interlock the pleats at the sides of the tail. Turn the paper over.

133 Fold the corners underneath. The next steps will focus on the head.

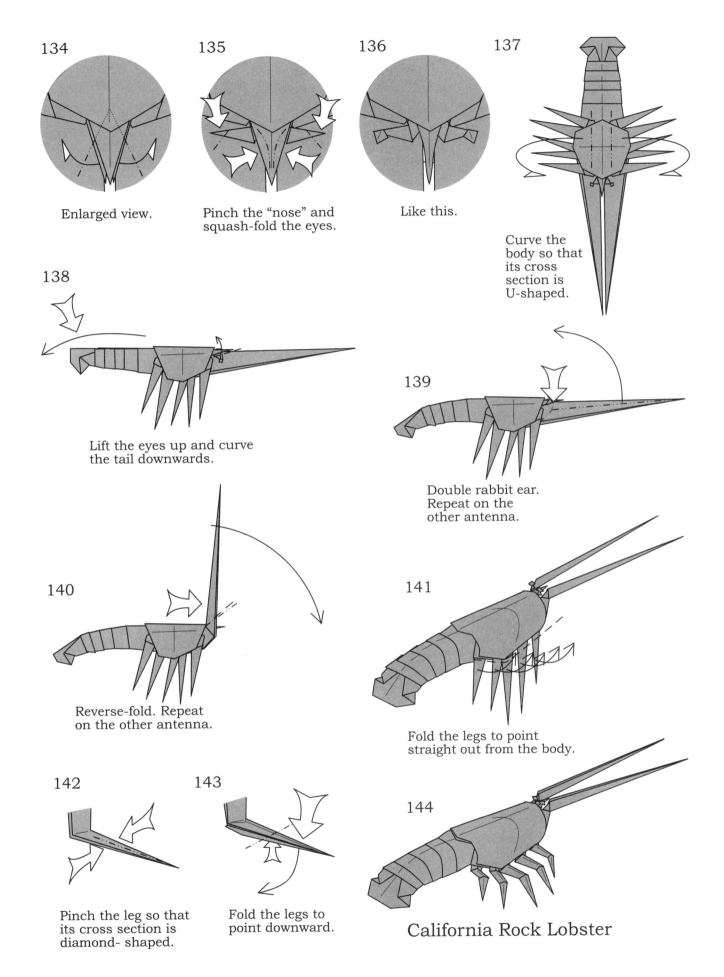

134

Enlarged view.

135

Pinch the "nose" and squash-fold the eyes.

136

Like this.

137

Curve the body so that its cross section is U-shaped.

138

Lift the eyes up and curve the tail downwards.

139

Double rabbit ear. Repeat on the other antenna.

140

Reverse-fold. Repeat on the other antenna.

141

Fold the legs to point straight out from the body.

142

Pinch the leg so that its cross section is diamond- shaped.

143

Fold the legs to point downward.

144

California Rock Lobster

Basic Folds

Rabbit Ear.

To fold a rabbit ear, one corner is folded in half and laid down to a side.

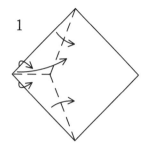

1

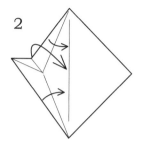

2

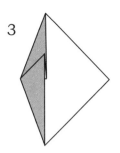

3

Fold a rabbit ear.

A 3D intermediate step.

Double Rabbit Ear.

If you were to bend a straw you would be folding the double rabbit ear.

1

2

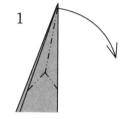

(Straw)

1

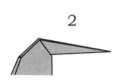

2

Make a double rabbit ear.

Squash Fold.

In a squash fold, some paper is opened and then made flat. The shaded arrow shows where to place your finger.

1

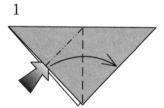

2

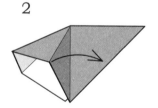

3

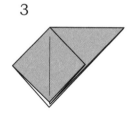

Squash-fold.

A 3D intermediate step.

Petal Fold.

In a petal fold, one point is folded up while two opposite sides meet each other.

1

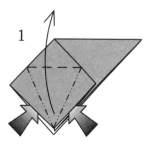

2

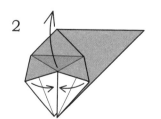

3

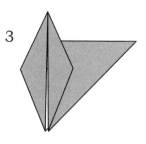

Petal-fold.

A 3D intermediate step.

Inside Reverse Fold.

In an inside reverse fold, some paper is folded between layers. Here are two examples.

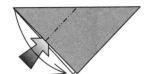

Reverse-fold.

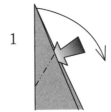

Reverse-fold.

Outside Reverse Fold.

Much of the paper must be unfolded to make an outside reverse fold.

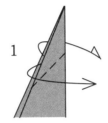

Outside-reverse-fold.

Crimp Fold.

A crimp fold is a combination of two reverse folds.

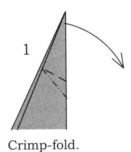

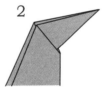

Crimp-fold.

Sink Fold.

In a sink fold, some of the paper without edges is folded inside. To do this fold, much of the model must be unfolded.

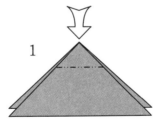

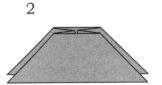

Sink.

Spread Squash Fold.

A cross between a squash fold and sink fold, some paper in the center is spread apart and then made flat.

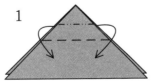

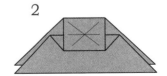

Spread-squash-fold.

Credits

The following models were designed by John Montroll:

Narwhal	Ocean Sunfish
Humpback Whale	Triggerfish
Dolphin	Cichlid
Octopus	Sailfish
Seahorse	Blue Shark
Parrotfish	Starfish

The following models were designed by Robert J. Lang:

Giant Clam	Sand Dollar
Murex	Atlantic Purple Sea Urchin
Chambered Nautilus Shell	Horseshoe Crab
Banded Angelfish	Hermit Crab
Hideko's Goldfish	Fiddler Crab
Blackdevil Angler	California Rock Lobster

Additional software used in the production of this book was written by Robert J. Lang.

The authors would like to acknowledge the contributions of several individuals who helped to bring about this book. Ron Levy and Terry Hall proofread the diagrams, catching many mistakes and making numerous helpful suggestions towards improving their clarity. Matt Harnick provided much of the zoological information about the different sea life. Barbara Hofer proofread the manuscript. Beth Panitz and Marjorie Wood helped with some of the text.